Historic ASPEN
in Rare Photographs

featuring
The Journals of Charles S. Armstrong

By Christian J. Buys

WESTERN REFLECTIONS PUBLISHING COMPANY

Ouray, Colorado

ii

Library of Congress Catalog Number 00-105542

ISBN 1-890437-31-X

Western Reflections Publishing Company
P.O. Box 710
Ouray, CO 81427

First Edition
Printed in the United States of America

Cover photograph: Courtesy of Ben Kirsten, see page 138
Cover inset photography: Front cover flap (Author's collection, see page 111), front cover (Author's photograph, see page 7), back cover flap (Colorado Historical Society, Stephen Hart Library, see page 37), back cover top and center (Beck family collection, see pages 187 and 217), lower back cover (Armstrong's journals, see page 156)

Cover and book design, typography and maps by Laurie Goralka Design

HISTORIC ASPEN IN RARE PHOTOGRAPHS

To Zachary Ekdal Buys and Stephen Christian Buys

❀

Acknowledgments

Larry Fredrick, a connoisseur of Aspen history and volunteer historian at the Aspen Historical Society, graciously reviewed all the captions, photographs, and maps for historical accuracy. Mining historian Leo Stambaugh drew my attention to the journals and photographs of Charles S. Armstrong. I cannot imagine having completed this endeavor without the help of these two fine friends. Thanks also to Laurie Goralka Casselberry for her exemplary art direction, design, and production. My wife, Beth VanKuiken Buys, and Rita Eisenheim provided excellent editorial suggestions.

Adeline Zupancis Kirsten and her son Ben Kirsten graciously shared a wealth of Aspen family photographs and memorabilia. Carol Beck Meachem and Mary Schaefer kindly allowed me to rephotograph numerous images in their Aspen family albums. I am also happy to acknowledge several other people who contributed to this endeavor: Barbara Bost, Rick Sinner, Tom Meachem, Gary Bracken, Ed Borasio, Ralph Kemper, Scott Strain, Bill Ellicott, Bruce McCallister, Hillary McCallister, Joann Leech, Jackie Broughton, Don Broughton, George Foott, Alfred Giles, Stacy Stambaugh, Elwood Gregory, Theresia Holman, and Katie Vining.

I owe special thanks to several people who helped me obtain copies of archival photographs: Lori Swingle (Denver Public Library, Western History Department), Nancy Manly (Colorado Mountain History Collection, Lake County Public Library), Daniel Davis (American Heritage Center, University of Wyoming), Judy Prosser-Armstrong (Museum of Western Colorado, Grand Junction, Colorado), Rebecca Lintz, Barbara Dey, and Debra Neiswonger (Stephen H. Hart Library, Colorado Historical Society), and Megan Harris (Aspen Historical Society). Some of the photographs that Charles S. Armstrong kept with this journals may have been taken by Drenkel Photography and itinerant photographer James "Horsethief" Kelley (see Landry and Lane, 1972).

I also gratefully acknowledge my good friends (and publishers) P. David and Jan Smith, who continue to amaze me with their boundless energy and enthusiasm for putting Colorado history in print.

Contents

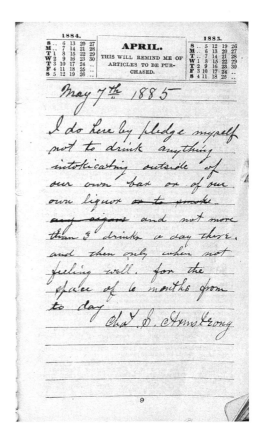

v

Aspen Regional Map

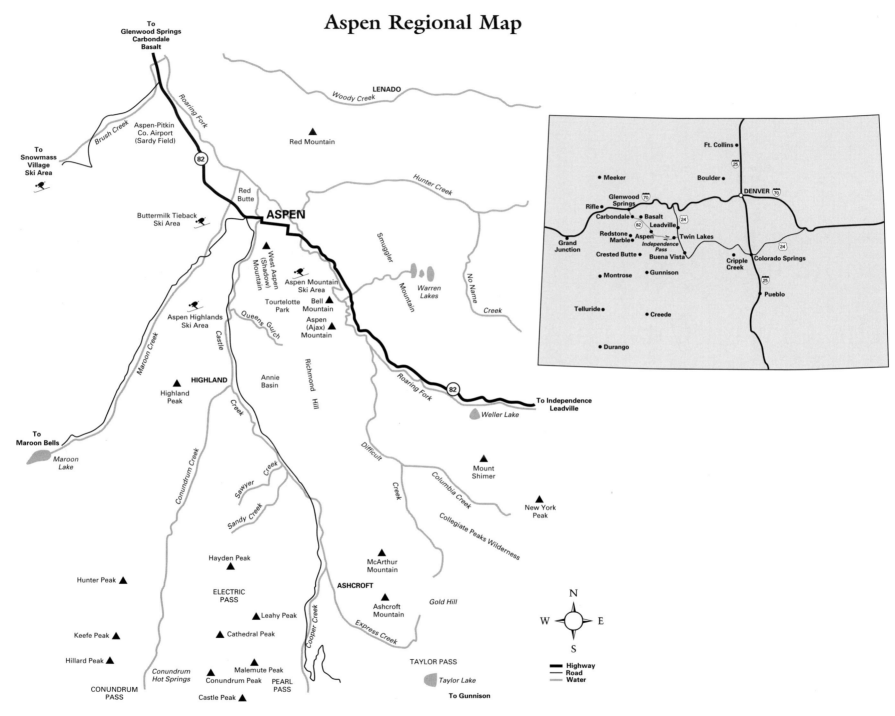

To
Glenwood Springs
Carbondale
Basalt

Roaring Fork

Brush Creek

Aspen-Pitkin
Co. Airport
(Sardy Field)

82

To
Snowmass
Village
Ski Area

Red Butte

Buttermilk Tieback
Ski Area

ASPEN

West Aspen
(Shadow)
Mountain

Aspen Mountain
Ski Area

Tourtelotte
Park

Bell
Mountain

Aspen
(Ajax)
Mountain

Aspen Highlands
Ski Area

Queens Gulch

Castle

Richmond Hill

Maroon Creek

HIGHLAND

Highland
Peak

Annie
Basin

To
Maroon Bells

Creek

Maroon
Lake

Conundrum Creek

Sawyer Creek

Sandy Creek

Hayden Peak

Hunter Peak

**ELECTRIC
PASS**

Keefe Peak

Leahy Peak

Cathedral Peak

Hillard Peak

Conundrum
Hot Springs

Malemute Peak

Conundrum Peak

**CONUNDRUM
PASS**

Castle Peak

Cooper Creek

**PEARL
PASS**

LENADO

Woody Creek

Red Mountain

Hunter Creek

Smuggler
Mountain

Warren
Lakes

No Name
Creek

Roaring Fork

82

To Independence
Leadville

Weller Lake

Difficult
Creek

Columbia Creek

Mount
Shimer

New York
Peak

Collegiate Peaks Wilderness

McArthur
Mountain

ASHCROFT

Ashcroft
Mountain

Gold Hill

Express Creek

TAYLOR PASS

Taylor Lake

To Gunnison

Ft. Collins

Meeker

Boulder

25

Glenwood
Springs

70

DENVER

70

Rifle

Carbondale

Basalt

24

Redstone
Marble

82

Leadville

Aspen

Twin Lakes

24

Grand
Junction

Independence
Pass

Crested Butte

Buena Vista

Cripple
Creek

Colorado Springs

Montrose

Gunnison

25

Telluride

Creede

Pueblo

Durango

N
W   E
S

Highway
Road
Water

vi

HISTORIC ASPEN IN RARE PHOTOGRAPHS

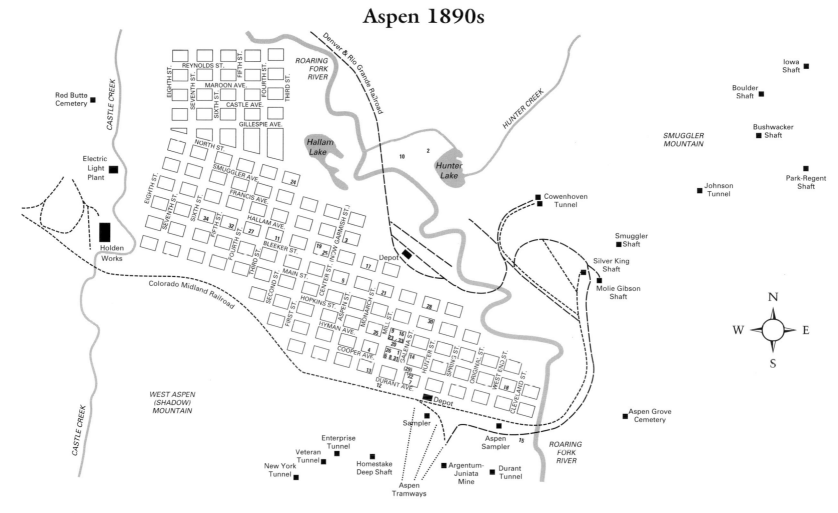

Aspen 1890s

1. Aspen Block
2. Aspen Citizens Hospital
3. Aspen High School (*formerly* D.C.R. Brown House)
4. *Aspen Times* Building
5. Atkinson House
6. Brick Saloon (*now* The Red Onion)
7. Brown and Hoag Block
8. Buckhorn Saloon
9. Carbary's Corner Bookstore
10. Chris Sander's Brewery
11. Christ Church
12. City Hall and Fire Station
13. Clarendon Hotel
14. Cowenhoven Building
15. Evergreen Cemetery (*now* Ute Cemetery)
16. First National Bank
17. First Presbyterian Church
18. Garfield School
19. Gillespie House
20. Hooper Brothers Jewelers
21. Hotel Jerome
22. Independence Building (Brown & Hoag)
23. Lamb's Drugstore
24. Lamb House
25. Lincoln School
26. McMillan Stock Brokers
27. Pioneer Park
28. Pitkin County Courthouse
29. Post Office
30. St. Mary's Catholic Church
31. Tomkins Hardware
32. Washington School
33. Wheeler Block
34. Wheeler-Stallard House Museum (*now* Aspen Historical Society)
35. Wheeler Opera House

HISTORIC ASPEN IN RARE PHOTOGRAPHS

Preface

Exalted Aspen. Tucked against the base of the majestic Rocky Mountains in central Colorado, Aspen rests on the south end of a dramatic alpine valley. Named the "Roaring Fork Valley" for the crystal rivers churning through it, few other valleys in Colorado can boast of such natural splendor. The glen's climate equals the beauty of its elevated setting. Under bright blue skies, mild summers complemented by bracing winters make resident and visitor alike happy to be alive. Hiking, biking, fishing, camping, skiing, and more are available in the Roaring Fork Valley and its surrounding foothills. In downtown Aspen, celebrities barely turn heads, while money abounds with shopping to match. As if this is not enough for a small mountain community, its cultural festivals and academic symposia attract international attention and attendance.

Then there is Aspen's fascinating history, the focus of this book. Although no settlers could have imagined that the foregoing descriptions would *ever* describe their remote mining camp, few would have denied that from its inception the "Crystal City" exuded a special air. As early as 1889, a prophetic reporter proclaimed that "Aspen was not, and probably never would be, a poor man's camp."

Centuries ago another people came to fish and hunt in what we Americans now call the Roaring Fork Valley. They, too, valued its breathtaking scenery and natural bounty. In the last quarter of the nineteenth century, however, it took yet another land-grab by mineral-crazed humans to wrest Aspen and vicinity from its rightful landlords, the Ute Indians. So goes the history of the American West.

There are several books about Aspen's intriguing history. My favorite is Malcolm J. Rohrbough's endeavor: *Aspen, The History of A Silver Mountain Town 1879 - 1893*. Rohrbough energizes Aspen's past with insightful cultural perspectives, intellectual honesty, and accurate historical details. Further, it is one of the best academic books that I have read on the history of any mining town in Colorado.

This book, *Historic Aspen in Rare Photographs,* as the title indicates, focuses on past images of Aspen. Fortunately, the unblinking eye of the camera has bequeathed to us a plethora of extraordinary photographs of the Crystal City and its inhabitants. Selecting images that best capture Aspen's historical essence proved to be challenging as well as fun.

During my search for images of historic Aspen, I made a serendipitous discovery that added a unique historical perspective to this book. In the early spring of 1999, I stopped to see a friend, Leo Stambaugh, in Georgetown, Colorado. I had called him earlier to ask for permission to photograph the Aspen artifacts in his store and small, yet impressive, museum. Leo graciously agreed to let me photograph any item that caught my eye. After I finished photographing a few artifacts,

he asked me if I wanted to look at something else. Behind the counter, on a stool, sat a cutoff cardboard box. From it protruded a set of small dusty journals and a tilted pile of curled, faded photographs. "What's this?" I inquired. Leo almost apologized. From the shoddy appearance of the materials I could understand why. He responded, "It's a set of old diaries, someone from the Aspen area."

I stared at the pocket-sized journals for a moment, then began to shuffle carefully through them like a deck of cards. Several of the covers had ornate handwritten dates from the 1890s and early 1900s. Better yet, a few of the calf-hide covers carried captivating folk art. If the content of these journals, I thought aloud, actually focused on Aspen, I could at least photograph this primitive, yet appealing art. It would add a personal dimension to the book. "Sure," Leo concurred, "just take them with you and return them when you're done." At first I hesitated, but I finally agreed to do so. I did not want to take all nineteen journals, so I selected four with the most decorative covers and six of the plain, older looking ones. I also borrowed several of the most intriguing photographs.

A few days later I lay on my living room couch browsing through one of the journals. I had selected a journal with a soft, reddish-colored cover and no date. Within minutes I found myself mesmerized by what I was reading. Could this be? In 1887 a man named Charles S. Armstrong had written almost daily accounts of his life while living in a small log cabin on Castle Creek in the foothills south of Aspen. He described prospecting, trapping, fishing, gardening, and myriads of other activities, including drinking. He mentioned the stagecoaches and people that passed by his cabin. He wrote about his walks to Ashcroft and Aspen. And comments were made on the weather, birds, animals, fellow prospectors, Indians, and local and national politics.

My heart began to race. I instinctively reached for the other journals, searching for an even earlier date. There was none, so I picked out a dark-covered journal dated 1912. I searched for two events: the fires that gutted the Wheeler Opera House (in Aspen) and the sinking of the *Titanic*. Sure enough, Armstrong mentioned both. That was it, I was hooked. I spent the next several evenings reading every word of each journal.

Then I began to hope. If the journals that I had left behind — the ones without the cover dates and folk art — happened to start before 1887 and *happened* to describe this young man's trip to Aspen, well, it would be special, very special. On my next trip to Denver I stopped in Georgetown and picked up the remaining journals. They were even better than I had dared imagine. Charles S. Armstrong began writing his dairy in 1867 in Arkport, New York. He scribbled his last entry in 1926 in Aspen. A record spanning nearly sixty years! Better yet, some of his most detailed and poignant descriptions focused on his journey west — from New York to Leavenworth, to Denver, to Leadville, and ultimately, to nascent Aspen. A true Aspen pioneer, Armstrong huddled in his tent in May 1880 and wrote impressions of his arduous trip over Hunter's Pass (near present-day Independence Pass) into the Roaring Fork Valley. As he passed through "Aspen and Roaring Fork City," he observed that there were no houses, only tents. He also mentions, nonchalantly, that he "surveyed" the new town of Highland (immediately south of Aspen). There's more, much more, but I will let you discover the highlights of this historically priceless set of "Aspen journals" as you turn the pages of this book.

1

CHAPTER ONE
Early Aspen (1870s-1880s)

Never mind the savages, the intimidating snow-capped mountains, or the forbidding remoteness — gold and silver abound! If you missed the California Gold Rush of '49, now is your chance. That is what many Americans heard and believed in 1859 when gold was first discovered along the eastern slope of the Rocky Mountains in Kansas Territory. Thousands of fortune seekers flocked to Denver City in present-day Colorado. Most left destitute, victims of land schemes and outlandish tales of mountains glittering with gold and silver. Some, however, stayed and continued to search. A few were rewarded with fairy-tale discoveries. With each new bonanza, fortune seekers flooded into places we now call Silver Plume, Central City, Black Hawk, Idaho Springs, Georgetown, and the biggest boom town of them all, Leadville.

Between 1860 and 1880 thousands of fortune seekers spread out across present-day Colorado. Viewed from above, this throng must have looked like an army of starving ants slowly surging into nearly impenetrable terrain. At first, small groups of prospectors groped their way along the unexplored contours of the Rocky Mountains. If they struck gold or silver, they stayed where they found it. A trickle of prospectors soon followed. Within months the trickle metamorphosed into a continuous line of fortune seekers and adventurers. Soon each discovery site became a thickly populated pocket of frenetic mining and mining-support activity. Once every inch of ground, or so it seemed, had been claimed, and once the mining camp started to mature into a town, restless souls seeking new discoveries headed over the next mountain range. So it was with the first prospectors to make the arduous journey into the distant valley of the roaring river.

They came from Leadville. In June 1879, Charles Bennett and three of his companions had had enough of the great, bustling boom town. Too many people and too few prospects. After gathering their supplies, Hayden survey maps, and courage, Bennett's small party probed west over the Sawatch Range and the Continental Divide. They struggled for days to reach the snow-covered crests. Then came the even tougher descent down the precipitous, craggy western slope. Bennett's party kept one eye on a churning river that they fittingly named the Roaring Fork, and with the other eye watched for hostile Utes. Finally, after over seventy miles of brutal travel, a pristine valley spread out before them.

The Roaring Fork River immediately swung north through the glen. Bennett and his three companions chose to go south across two incredibly high-banked creeks (now called Castle and Maroon) into an open meadow. To their astonishment, they were greeted by another group of prospectors, who were equally taken aback to see them. Philip Pratt and his two companions had also travelled from Leadville, although by way of Gothic to the south. For over a week they had been searching for silver at the base of Aspen Mountain, one of the four mountains bordering the south end of the valley.

These two intrepid parties concluded that the picturesque area held enough riches for both of them. They decided to cooperate instead of fight. According to most historians, the euphoric Pratt group left for

5573. Aspen, Col. U. S, A.

Leadville early the next morning to file on two rich silver claims — the Spar and Pioneer (also called Galena) — at the foot of Aspen Mountain. The Bennett party remained another five days. They meticulously searched the entire south end of the valley for promising geological features at the base of the mountains. Before leaving for Leadville, they painstakingly staked out seven silver outcroppings on Aspen Mountain, West Aspen Mountain, and Smuggler Mountain. On their way back to Leadville to file their claims, dreams of wealth danced in Bennett's and his companions' heads.

No one could keep such a strike secret in Leadville. Before the short high-country summer ended in 1879, more parties set out for the pristine valley of the Roaring Fork River. Among the first was a group led by Henry B. Gillespie, who would become a major figure in shaping Aspen's rich destiny. He staked several more claims, supposedly jumped a few abandoned ones, and named the ramshackle collection of tents in the meadow, "Ute City." But Gillespie did not stay. Before deep snow made crossing the Sawatch Range impossible, he and his party headed back to Leadville for the winter. Only a few hardy, some said foolish, men chose to remain at their diggings near Ute City.

B. Clark Wheeler, another Leadville resident and shrewd entrepreneur, could not bear to wait for the spring of 1880 to seek his fortune in Ute City. He outfitted his small party with long Norwegian skis known as "snowshoes," and in mid-February made a mad winter dash for the riches of the Roaring Fork Valley. Upon his unexpected arrival, Wheeler surveyed tiny Ute City, then arbitrarily changed its name to Aspen. Come spring a steady stream of prospectors, including Charles S. Armstrong, trudged over Hunter's Pass (soon called Independence Pass) to Aspen. Historians often claim that these mineral-crazed pilgrims did not take the time to admire their surroundings. As you will read, Charles Armstrong's journals prove otherwise.

Men backed by money, like B. Clark Wheeler and Charles A. Hallam, and soon men *with* money, like Jerome B. Wheeler (no relation) and David M. Hyman, started Aspen on a course followed by many mountain boom towns. Thanks to capitalists willing to risk large sums, within a few years some of the mines started paying off. With money flowing in Aspen, wooden houses soon replaced tents and log cabins, churches outnumbered brothels, schools filled with children, and samplers spewed pollution. A first-class hotel, brick and sandstone opera house, and modern volunteer fire station sporting a distinctive bell tower sprouted quickly and became familiar landmarks. Downtown, successful businesses lined the dirt streets from one end to the other. Still, because of its remote location and the formidable mountain barriers on its eastern perimeter, it took several years for Aspen to reach the pinnacle of its mining-town glory. Finally, after the railroads arrived in the late 1880s, the Crystal City blossomed into a silver-mining Mecca rivaled by few others in America.

By 1889 Aspen had become a bustling, full-blown mining community with a population pushing 10,000. Besides the Colorado Midland and the Denver and Rio Grande Railroads, it boasted five smelters, a hydroelectric power plant, several churches, a full range of municipal buildings and services, a centerpiece courthouse, and several elegant brick homes. Of course, Aspen was not without its saloons and red light district, although from the very beginning it gained the reputation of being one of the most family-oriented and cultured camps in Colorado.

3

A. B. W. 1889 ASPEN Col.

HENRY BECK, ASPEN. - . COLORADO

They lost more than their land

For centuries Ute Indians roamed throughout present-day Colorado. During summer small groups of Utes established hunting camps near Conundrum Hot Springs above Aspen. Other groups hunted, fished, and foraged in the pristine Roaring Fork Valley. Come winter, they returned to their camps in the lower valleys. Today many people characterize this lifestyle as idyllic and environmentally friendly.

In the latter half of the nineteenth century, however, the Utes lost more than their land. Mineral-crazed, land-hungry fortune seekers flooded into the West, leaving a trail of broken treaties, dead buffalo, and disease-decimated Indians. Once characterized as the "Great Movement West," it is now described in genocidal terms (*The Earth Shall Weep*, 1999). By the 1870s many Utes in Colorado Territory had already been forcibly moved onto reservations. The Indians shown here in the 1860s and 1870s are at the Los Pinos Agency, a reservation established for bands of Utes in southern Colorado. (Both from Colorado Historical Society, Stephen Hart Library)

5

The Utes Must Go.

But don't forget to patronize the Pioneer Grocery of Colorado.
WOLFE LONDONER.

"The Utes Must Go"

By the late 1870s, silver and gold camps peppered the new state of Colorado's landscape. Leadville reigned as the biggest and boldest camp. Located in the Arkansas Valley between the spectacular Mosquito and Sawatch Mountain Ranges, it overflowed with thousands of fortune seekers. In the spring of 1879 small parties of fortune seekers left Leadville and made their way west over the Sawatch Range into the Roaring Fork Valley. After locating several promising silver-ore formations, they christened their tiny tent-settlement "Ute City."

In early October 1879, Ute City prospectors fled back to Leadville because of an outbreak among its namesake Indian tribe. On September 29, 1879, the Utes had attacked an army command that entered their reservation less than twenty miles from the White River Agency in north-central Colorado — and less than a two day ride from Ute City. At the agency they slaughtered Nathan Meeker, the controversial and puritanical Indian agent. A state-wide "Indian alert" went out. Governor Frederick W. Pitkin announced that unless removed by the government, the Utes "must necessarily be exterminated." Even business ads in Denver newspapers (left) played on Coloradans' fear and loathing of the Utes. (Colorado Historical Society, Stephen Hart Library).

Of the Ute City denizens' retreat to Leadville 1879, *The Daily Chronicle* wrote: "THE miners who took refuge in Leadville from anticipated Ute troubles in the Gunnison country [included Ute City in present-day Pitkin County], announce it to be their purpose to return 'healed' for any emergency. They will hereafter bear steadily in mind the fact that Colorado's Governor has declared it to be the duty of frontier settlers to treat as wild beasts all Indians found away from the reservation" (October 11, 1879).

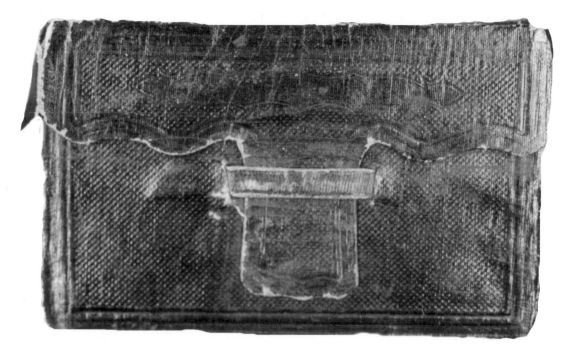

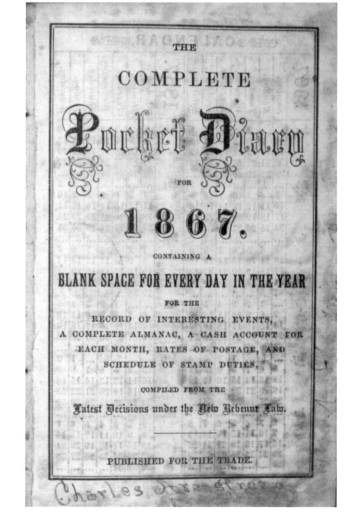

The journals of Charles S. Armstrong

Twelve years before the Ute uprising, twenty-year-old Charles Armstrong penned the first entry in his journal in rural Arkport, New York. It had been less than two years since General Robert E. Lee surrendered to General Ulysses S. Grant at Appomattox. Leadville and Aspen did not exist. Like thousands of young men and women in the eastern United States, Armstrong dreamed of going "West," to the land of opportunity. Bored with his bland, impoverished life in rural New York, Armstrong finally took the leap in 1878.

Unlike thousands of other young men and women, Armstrong kept a written record of his odyssey. That these historically intriguing documents have survived is reward enough for any person interested in the history of the American West. That Armstrong's destiny led him to Aspen is more than any person interested in Colorado history could ask. Shown here is his first small calf-hide journal.

Armstrong's accounts are presented here with minimal annotation. For ease of reading, some punctuation, capitalization, and paragraphing have been reluctantly added. Further, since the author agrees with William Unrau (1979) "that punctuating and syntax for a particular period are of more than casual interest," few major editorial changes have been made. (Armstrong's journals)

Armstrong drew, too

S ketches of Armstrong's family farm, a favorite childhood retreat, and possibly a self-portrait, adorn his early journals. (Armstrong's journals)

THE LEAVENWORTH TIMES.

CLARKE, EMERY & CO. }
Publishers and Proprietors.
LEAVENWORTH, THURSDAY MORNING, AUGUST 22, 1867. { VOLUME XVI. NUMBER 1-8.

BUTTERFIELD'S OVERLAND MAIL-COACH STARTING OUT FROM ATCHISON, KANSAS.—[SKETCHED BY WILLIAM M. MERRICK.]

Kansas

Not every pilgrim who traveled to the "border state" of Kansas immediately continued west. During his second journey "through" Kansas, Charles Armstrong worked as a night clerk at the Continental Hotel in bustling Leavenworth from October 1878 to May 1880. He received twenty dollars a month and board.

Before railroads stetched west of the Missouri River in the late 1860s, thousands of fortune seekers and immigrants rode Butterfield's Overland stages (above) from Kansas to Denver, Colorado Territory. (Masthead: *The Leavenworth Times*, August 22, 1867) (*Harper's Weekly*, January 27, 1866)

"Men searching for silver"

While Armstrong lingered in Leavenworth, Leadville boomed and Aspen was born. An early *Harper's Weekly* (January 19, 1889) recalled: "On the western slope of the Continental Divide, among nameless mountain-peaks and lonely canons, men were searching for silver in the early summer of 1880. Leadville was dull. The great carbonate camp had touched the farthest edge of its field of riches, and had turned back upon itself to ask the gruesome question, 'After this, what?' Only too ready to foresee for Leadville a place in the ghostly procession of dead camps and unrealized hopes, a number of prospectors climbed the snowy heights of Mount Massive and pushed out into the unknown country beyond, to begin anew their unrewarded search for wealth." (Crofutt, 1881)

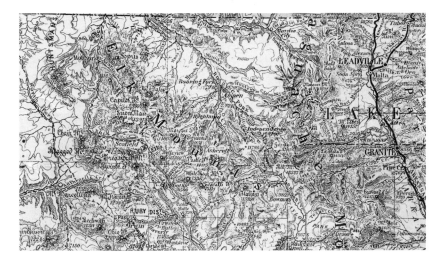

Hayden's Survey

During 1879 and 1880 men like Phillip W. Pratt, Smith Steele, Charles E. Bennett, Henry B. Gillespie, and B. Clark Wheeler led the first small prospecting parties into the Roaring Fork Valley. All of them carried maps featuring geological features. These invaluable travel and prospecting guides resulted from previous Hayden surveys (above). Colorado survey groups, like the one shown here, had to leave their wagons behind in the rugged region of the Roaring Fork. In the 1870s, the Utes reluctantly allowed the government-sponsored Hayden group to map huge areas of uncharted Colorado Territory.

Harper's Weekly (January 19, 1889) spared few superlatives while reporting on the activities of these early prospectors: "In this Rocky Mountain country there are deeds of daring that go unrecorded; there are tales of heroism that never get beyond the four walls of a miner's cabin; and there are agonies of suffering that pass unnoticed and unknown . . . . Perilous journeys and hazardous deeds are so common in the Rocky Mountains, and men there are so prone to underrate anything within the every-day scope of their own lives, that many, no doubt, will wonder what there could be in a walk of forty miles over the mountains to excite comment" (*Harper's Weekly*, October 12, 1878). (Crofutt, 1881)

11

"All honor to the ladies of Aspen"

*I*n Leadville, during the late summer of 1879, mining entrepreneur Henry B. Gillespie learned about Pratt's and Steele's new claims in the Roaring Fork Valley. He saw an opportunity. Sight unseen he purchased (with the financial backing of casket and mining magnate Abel D. Breed) options on the Spar and Galena claims on Aspen Mountain for $25,000. Wasting no time, Gillespie made the arduous trip over the Continental Divide with his wife and about a dozen Leadville miners to begin developing his properties. Almost immediately he spearheaded a meeting to organize the camp, naming it "Ute City" (the next summer B. Clark Wheeler's controversial Aspen Town and Land Company changed it to "Aspen").

According to the first issue of *The Aspen Times* (April 23, 1881), Mrs. Henry B. Gillespie (right) was one of the few women "who remained in camp during the long and dreary winter of '80 and '81. All honor to the ladies of Aspen." Mrs. Gillespie also helped organize the first literary club, a Sabbath school, musicals, dances, and even a Temperance Union, setting a high cultural tone in Aspen. Of Aspen's early social scene *Harper's Weekly* proclaimed: "Even in the early days of its career, Aspen never had much of this law-breaking element . . . and the comparative nearness of Leadville as a centre of criminal disturbance, prevented a dangerous assembling of objectionable characters in the valley of the Roaring Fork" (January 19, 1889). (Aspen Historical Society)

B. Clark Wheeler

B. Clark Wheeler, a Leadville resident and shrewd entrepreneur, could not bear to wait for the spring of 1880 to seek his fortune in Ute City. He outfitted his small party with skis and in mid-February made a perilous winter dash for the silver-rich Roaring Fork Valley. *Harper's Weekly* (January 19, 1889) recounted this legendary trek: "The Saguache [Sawatch] Range was a solid wall of snow; the mountain passes were blocked with huge drifts; storms were howling and shrieking through the narrow canons, and snow-slides were coasting down the rocky steeps; yet he set out . . . . After several days of desperate struggle with the cold and snow, this adventurous man reached the new camp. Soon afterward he measured off in the snow the streets and building lots of a new town. This was the beginning of the rich young city of Aspen, the metropolis of the Roaring Fork, and the financial rival of Leadville. It was a profitable walk for the venturesome town-builder, since to-day Mr. B. Clark Wheeler is proprietor of the *Aspen Daily Times,* and the manager and controlling power of a number of rich and extensive mining properties. Most men would have waited until the snow had disappeared from the mountain passes in the spring before attempting a pilgrimage to the camp on the Roaring Fork. It is one thing to have foresight, and a valuable thing, too, in its way, but it is quite another matter to have the pluck and energy with which to back it up." (Aspen Historical Society)

13

Independence Pass and Independence

14

During 1879, most of the fortune seekers who entered the Roaring Fork Valley struggled over the Continental Divide via 12,095 foot-high Independence Pass (also known as Hunter's Pass). After a series of hair-raising switchbacks, the primitive trail to Aspen snaked through the small settlement of Independence. Traditional wisdom holds that on July 4, 1879, two lucky prospectors discovered gold high in the upper valley of the Roaring Fork and named the site after the holiday.

By 1880 over 300 people called Independence (also listed in State Business Directories as Chipeta and Sparkill) their home. By 1881 a stage service (see page 59) from Leadville to Aspen made a regular stop at Independence. In the summer of 1883 the population swelled to 1,500, nearly double that of Aspen's. With over forty businesses, a stamp mill, a post office, and a newspaper, Independence justifiably felt like the king of the mountains. Within a few years, however, the lure of Aspen's rich silver strikes, plentiful job opportunities, lower elevation, milder climate, train service, and urban amenities slowly drained the life out of Independence. By the turn of the century (left), only deforested slopes and dilapidated buildings served as reminders of the once-promising gold camp. (Colorado Historical Society, Stephen Hart Library)

Armstrong arrives in Leadville

*I*n May 1880, after spending a year and a half as a hotel night clerk in Leavenworth, Kansas, Charles Armstrong finally overcame his internal struggles and took the leap. He left his safe haven and headed west. He boarded the train in Leavenworth, riding the rails to Denver and Buena Vista. He arrived in Leadville — the boom town of boom towns — on May 9, 1880. Another first-time visitor observed: "We could look up its [Chestnut Street, shown above] length, possible [sic] two miles. It was a crawling mass of horses, mules, wagons, and men. It looked impossible to get through, but we made it in about two hours" (quoted in Blair, 1980).

Armstrong did not linger in Leadville. Within weeks he struck out for a new, more promising mining camp across the Continental Divide in the Roaring Fork Valley. (*Frank Leslie's Illustrated Newspaper*, April 12, 1879)

Sunday, May 16, 1880: Left Leadville yesterday about noon for 'Roaring Forks'

rmstrong's diary entries from May 16, 1880 through May 25, 1880, comprise an extraordinary firsthand account of a novice prospector — though bonded surveyor — crossing the formidable Continental Divide and descending into the isolated, newly founded mining camp of Aspen, Colorado. Shown here are two original pages of the journal that Armstrong kept with him during his passage. Years later Armstrong traced his pencil entries in ink. (Armstrong's journals)

16

Over the Range to Aspen City and Highland

Sunday, May 16, 1880 There are a few houses and a store & Post Office here [Twin Lakes]. I wrote a letter home today. We are having very fine weather and I don't like to be laying around, but have to wait on the others.

Tuesday, May 18, 1880. I am in camp at Seaden's Ranch [soon a regular stage stop] about 10 miles from Twin Lakes and about 5 from the top of the Range, where we have to cross. I am waiting till the boys come back. They have gone on to the foot of the range about 4 miles with half the stuff and are coming back for the remainder. The road is bad and they have to double back. We left Twin Lakes yesterday about 10 o'clock and came to this place and camped for the night. I did not feel very well yesterday or last night. And I was very much afraid that I was going to be sick, but I feel pretty good this morning. There are lots of people going by this morning bound for Roaring Forks. There is lots of snow all around here. I am sitting within 10 feet of a big snowbank.

Wednesday, May 19, 1880. I am in camp waiting for the boys to get back. They have gone over the summit with part of the stuff. We have to double back till we get over the Range. It is about 2 miles to the summit by the trail, and about a mile straight over. The snow is 8 & 10 feet deep in places.

Thursday, May 20, 1880. We camped on the summit of the range above timberline. Had a very rough time of it. The snow on the summit is from 3 to 12 feet deep, where the trail is shoveled out. We had a snow storm of about 1/2 hours duration. I slept very cold and did not rest worth a cent last night. This morning I saw a couple of mountain quail. Shot at one but did not kill him. They are white as snow and about as large as partridge. We have had a hard time today getting down off the range. We had to carry everything down the mountain. The jacks could not carry their loads on account of the steepness of the mountain and also the snow. The snow is about 5 feet deep here in the woods. Some good pine timber here — trees 18 inches through.

Saturday, May 22, 1880 [no entry on May 21]. Nooning on the North Fork of Roaring Fork River. Yesterday, we left our camp at the foot of the Range and doubled to Seaden's Ranch where we left some of our stuff. Was delayed there for a couple of hours by a snow storm. Camped at night about 1 1/2 miles below Seadan's. Had a nice camp. Cut pine boughs and made a fine bed. There is much more snow on this side of the Range than the other. Camped tonight near the North Fork of Roaring Fork in the timber. Had a hard afternoon. Trail very muddy & bad. [Oddly, Armstrong never mentions the settlement of Independence.]

Sunday, May 23, 1880. We left camp early this morning and had about 400 yds to go to North Fork, where we had to cross on a Jack Bridge — three trees felled across the river and pine bows put on and covered with dirt. We had to unpack our jacks and carry our things across. Had dinner, then we had to carry our stuff about 1/2 mile through the snow. I saw some kind of a wild animal today. I did not know if it was a young bear or a wolverine. Well, we finally got a very good trail and got to the Forks of Roaring Forks, where we had to cross again. Carried our stuff over on a foot log and drove the jacks through. Camped on the banks of the river. The river is about 4 rods wide below the forks and very swift.

Monday, May 24, 1880. Left camp before breakfast and traveled about 2 miles over a very bad trail, muddy and lots of fallen timber. Found some grass for the jacks and stopped for breakfast. [In the] afternoon we had a good trail. Travelled about 4 miles and are camped on the level with fine grass. There are some small lakes here, originally beaver dams. The mountains are very high and rocky here. The scenery along Roaring Forks is grand.

Thursday, May 25, 1880. We pulled out from camp early this morning. Had a good trail all day. We crossed Roaring Forks on a jack bridge. Paid our toll in bacon, 5 lbs at 30¢ pr pound, 25¢ a jack. The bridge is a big pine with two smaller on each side. We passed through the City of Aspen, crossed Castle Creek, and passed through the City of Roaring Forks. Not a house in either town. They have a fine location, a fine level bottom, and no timber. We camped for the night on Castle Creek about 4 miles from Highland, a mining town where we are going to locate. Snowing this evening. (Armstrong's journals)

A miner's cabin near Aspen

*T*his illustration is featured in an early *Harper's Weekly* article entitled "The City of Aspen, Colorado." The writer observed: "The circumstances of the miner's life, too, tend to make him practical and indifferent to the artistic features of his environment. The rude cabin in the lonely cañon, the rough couch of spruce boughs, the unpalatable fare, the remoteness of the refining influence of civilization, and the daily toil in shafts and tunnels that may contain nothing worth the seeking, leave their finger-touches on the heart in characters that never grow dim. I never have met the drunken, reckless, murderous desperado that the East has conjured up from its imagination, but I have met plenty of honest, hard-working, educated men in the Small Hopes at Leadville, and in the Iowa and Johnston mines at Aspen, who would do credit to any community of the conservative East." (*Harper's Weekly,* January 19, 1889)

Waiting, Rotgut, and Excitement in Aspen

Thursday, July 8, 1880. Sitting in our cabin, just had dinner . . . Schlag [Armstrong's friend] *and I just moved off the hill down to the town of Highland and have built a house. Schlag left here 3 weeks ago today and went to Leadville after provisions, but he has failed to get back. I have been expecting him every day. I have not done anything in the surveying line. When we came down here the town was lively and full of people but — now there is but a very few in town and there is nothing doing. The 4th I spent here doing nothing, managed to get pretty full of rotgut which made me very sick. The next morning I threw up about a pint of gall which did me lots of good. I have felt much better ever since. There is considerable excitement down in Aspen City — there has been some good strikes made down there. One mine, the Smuggler, was sold a short time ago for 165,000 dollars.*
(Armstrong's journals)

19

Armstrong's cabin on Castle Creek

Surely Armstrong fit in the "honest, hard-working, educated men" category. In the early 1880s Armstrong built a cabin on Castle Creek between Highland and Ashcroft. In the 1890s he built a larger one (above). On the back of this photograph he wrote: *Charles Torry in front of my cabin with our horses and dog.* Like many prospectors, Armstrong established small prospecting "camps" within about a fifteen-mile radius of his cabin. Imagine spending high-country winters in these crude log cabins. (Armstrong's journals)

20

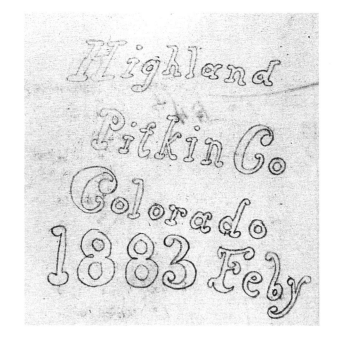

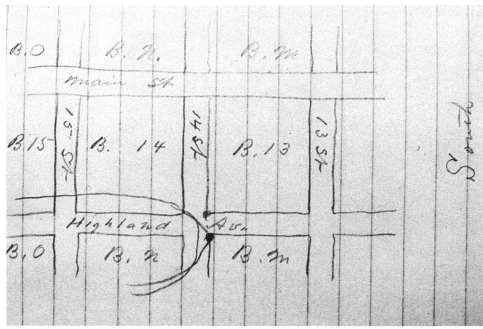

Highland

Located about six miles above Aspen at the confluence of Conundrum Creek and Castle Creek, Highland never amounted to much. Little is known of its history. No map of the site is known. Yet Charles Armstrong attended "miners' meetings" in Highland as early as June 1880. Quickly, they hired him to survey the town for a generous $100 retainer. It took him three days. His rare, rough sketch of Highland is shown above.

Three years later Armstrong still considered himself a Highland resident (left). In 1886 the Colorado State Business Directory listed Highland as: "A small camp in Pitkin County; Population 10; Post Office at Aspen." (Both from Armstrong's journals)

Ashcroft

L ocated about 12 miles above Aspen on Castle Creek, Ashcroft (also known as Castle Forks City and Chloride) rivaled Aspen in 1880. This is a view of a false-front business in Ashcroft. Men are sitting and standing on the front boardwalk while another man loads his horse with supplies.

Like Independence, many people felt Ashcroft held great promise as a mining camp. But, like Independence, it was not to be. By 1881 a popular tourist guide (Crofutt, 1881) reported: "Ashcroft — Gunnison county, is situated twelve miles south from Aspen, on Castle Creek, and forty-five miles west from Leadville, by trail. It is a small mining camp, and shows some rich 'prospects,' but no developments." Another part of the problem can be inferred from the 1883 Colorado State Business Directory that gave Ashcroft's population as "summer, 1,000; winter, uncertain." By 1885 Ashcroft's population dropped below 100. It simply could not compete with all Aspen had to offer. (Denver Public Library, Western History Department)

21

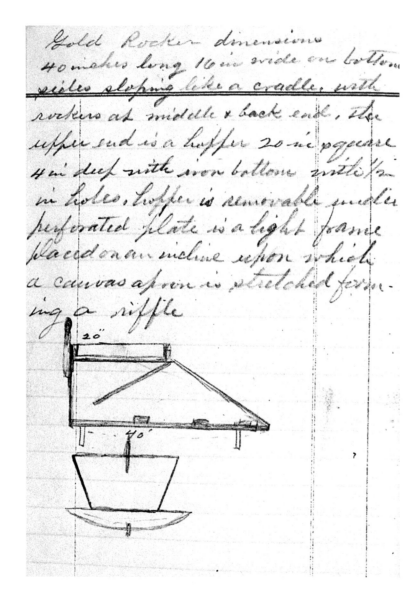

Rich mines "worth no more than common dirt"

*I*n their initial quest for wealth, many prospectors built, bought, or bartered for a rocker. Armstrong must have copied these rocker instructions and plans (left) from a mining journal or manual. For processing "free standing" gold, rockers ranked a step above gold pans, though several below sluices. Only Independence yielded gold. In the Aspen and Ashcroft vicinity most early prospectors spent more time looking for rich silver-ore formations than for gold nuggets.

Yet finding silver-bearing ore was only the first step. *Harper's Weekly* proclaimed: "There are plenty of rich silver mines in Colorado worth no more than common dirt. The men who carried the pick, the shovel, and the blow-pipe into this Western wilderness apparently cared but little for the availability of their discoveries, as they were just as ready to locate claims on the tops of towering mountains as on the gentlest hillside. They held to the miner's common fallacy that wherever precious metals can be dug out or ground or blasted out of rock, a way will be found to transport it to market. In this case a way was found, undoubtedly, but it came only after years of patient waiting" (January 19, 1889). (Armstrong's journals)

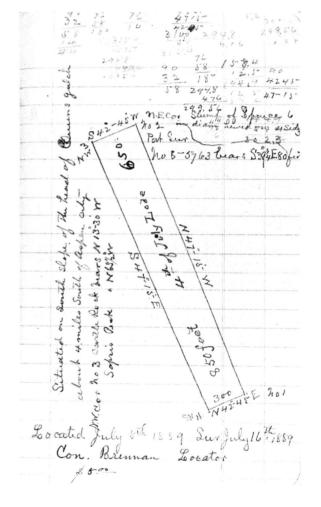

Legal claims required accurate surveys

Without a legal claim and a proper survey, prospectors risked losing their discoveries. Typical claims usually measured 300 feet x 1,500 feet. For a claim to be patented a legal survey had to be filed at the county clerk's office. Claim owners also had to prove that they spent more than $100 on "improvements" each year and extended a shaft or tunnel at least 10 feet. Shown here are two of Armstrong's surveys from the late 1880s. He usually charged $5 to $10 a survey, depending on the difficulty of terrain and the distance traveled from his cabin on Castle Creek. Legalities aside, prospectors often found their claims "jumped" by unscrupulous fortune seekers. Thus the wave of attorneys that surged into mining camps on the heals of the prospectors. (Both from Armstrong's journals)

Hard labor

*I*n remote, isolated mountain regions like Aspen, early prospectors extracted ore by their own hard labor. To get the ore to the smelters they had to pack it out by "jack trains" or have it "teamed [freighted]" on treacherous trails over the Continental Divide to Leadville. Although many prospectors would have disagreed, an early mining publication wrote: "For the first seven years of Aspen's existence, its inaccessibility prevented that rush which usually is a great detriment to most new mining camps . . . . The result has been a steady, substantial growth and a gradual opening up of its resources that has kept pace with the increase in population" (Canfield, 1893). (Crane, 1913)

24

Next came longer tunnels, surface structures, and mining equipment

*I*f the silver-ore vein kept going, miners followed it. As a matter of necessity and convenience miners usually erected a cabin and tool shed near the mine entrance. In tunnels miners installed mining tracks for ore carts. For shafts they installed windlasses and ore buckets.

In this unidentified photograph miners sit on a pile of cut lumber. Directly behind them is an ore cart. The mining-car tracks lead to a sturdy wooden structure that appears to be a loading bin. A small pyramid of bulging ore bags can be seen behind the two men on the left. (Armstrong's journals)

Mr. Bear and Winter in Leadville

Thursday, October 14, 1880. Camped at Highland on the hill. We left Spring Creek a week ago today. Got in here on Friday. Went into camp and covered up our claims and fixed them for winter, except the Baer Lode which we put a windlass on and cleaned out. We would have been done, but the weather has been very bad. We have about a foot of snow and it has been storming for a week, besides, we have spent 3 days hunting our jack Jerry. Found him once, but Tuesday morning he left again with one of Beebee's mules. A bear stampeded them. But Tuesday morning some miners working on the Eva Belle Mine caught and killed Mr. Bear. They built a log trap and baited it with fresh meat. Mr Bear went in and did not come back alive. I have killed two deer, one fine buck and a doe, and a rabbit and grouse in the past week, so we have plenty of meat.

Friday, November 26, 1880. Am in the city of Leadville once more. We arrived in town two weeks ago today. We were the last ones to leave Highland. (Armstrong's journals)

25

In a Bushwhacker stope

*I*n this underground room, or stope, two Bushwhacker miners (in a later photograph) are using small sledge hammers and short steel bits to knock off ore hunks. Another miner waits to shovel the hunks into an ore cart. Candles provide the only light. There is nothing adventuresome or glorious about working in dark, dank, and dangerous stopes. The Bushwhacker was located on Smuggler Mountain about one mile east of Aspen. (Lake County Public Library)

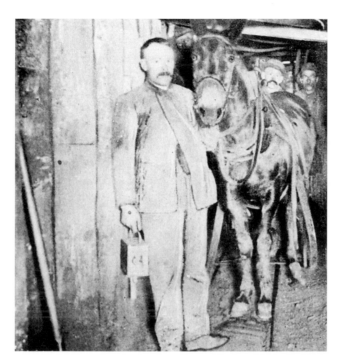

Beasts of burden

*I*gnore the cute-sounding propaganda about burros in this early Aspen business brochure. Many burros spent their entire lives laboring in underground mines. They often went blind. (Lake County Public Library) (Aspen Commercial Club)

The Burro.

The little burro is typical of all the Rocky Mountain country, and he is found in Aspen in abundance. Patient, self-contained long-suffering and kind, he has proved himself of great value to the men who work in mines where only steep and rugged trails lead to the workings. He is a godsend to the miner and prospector, and a useful addition to a party of tourists.

Aspen, Colorado.

Offers varied lines of investments for capital and attractive resorts for pleasure seekers. For information address

THE ASPEN COMMERCIAL CLUB,
ASPEN, COLORADO.

Photographs by courtesy of John Bowman.

Tourtelotte Park

*H*enry Tourtelotte founded this small mining settlement (top left) on Aspen Mountain in 1879. At its height Tourtelotte Park boasted a population of 500, although early map makers (bottom left) ignored it. In 1909 (below), "Irving Adams, Dorothy Adams, Lucile Adams, Greeners, [and] Uncle Joe Tourtelotte" pose next to wildflowers in front of Uncle Joe's log cabin.

Nothing remains of this small camp, except a ski run with same name. (Aspen Historical Society) (Denver Public Library, Western History Department) (Crofutt, 1885)

28

Great Ore Bin of the Durant Compromise Co., Aspen

DENVER PHOTO SUPPLY CO.

Eastern capital and mining litigation

Absentee mine owners and disputes over mining claims fueled debates in mining camps throughout Colorado. Aspen was no exception. Eastern capitalist David M. Hyman, along with his point-man and partner Charles A. Hallam, held controlling interest in several Aspen mines, including the rich Smuggler and Durant (its ore bins shown here). Some locals felt resident owners better served the needs of the community, but residents rarely had the money necessary to develop the mines. Other locals actively pursued eastern capital, believing that Aspen could not survive without it.

As for mining and litigation, they were inseparable. Hardly a claim was filed, or a wheel barrel of ore extracted, without someone contesting something. It was always about money. The Spar Mine is a good example. Once the Spar started to show rich silver ore, Pratt and Steele claimed fraud and disputed Gillespie's and Breed's ownership. A protracted court battle ensued. All mining operations ceased. Everyone suffered financially. (Lake County Public Library)

29

Weather, An Irresponsible Friend, Aspen Reduction Works, an Election

Sunday, September 6, 1885. Stormy day. Pete & Bill Paine [?] down today. They are 162 feet in the tunnel & have not struck it yet. Got dinner for 7.

Saturday, September 19, 1885. Got out 5 1/2 this morning. [Had] 6 for breakfast. Fine clear morning. Schlag went to Aspen last Tuesday with 55 dollars cash and has not got back yet. I suppose he has blowed it all in and all that he could collect beside. Pete and Bill went on the hill to work on their tunnel again. Bill has been to town since last Sunday on a drunk.

Sunday, September 20, 1885. Got out 5 1/2 this morning. [Had] 4 for breakfast. Fine clear day. I hear this morning that the Union Pacific R.R. have contracted to freight 15,000 tons of ore to St. Elmo, which will all go by hire, meaning a good road and trade for us all winter. Also, they are going to build big reduction works in Aspen, which is a good thing for this country, as the smelter has everything their own way now. I just hope it is all true. The stage was filled with passengers this morning. A big 42 horse power boiler & machinery went down this morning for the Enterprise Tunnel.

Friday, October 2, 1885. Got out at 5.45 this morning. [Had] 5 here for S & B [sleep and breakfast?]. Schlag got home last Monday night after spending 75 dollars. He went to town again last night after a team. Took $10 with him. He is getting more no account every year. He is lazier than any body.

Tuesday, November 3, 1885. Election day. I went to town to the Election. Schlag went down yesterday. I stopped in town all night. Did not go to bed at all. Won $20.00 at faro. Came home on the stage Wednesday morning.

Saturday, March 13, 1886. Fine day. It has been very storm weather for the past week. I went to Aspen Sunday evening after provisions. Stayed till Thursday morning. Pete was down Sunday. They are in 315 feet in the tunnel. Schlag has been up there for 2 weeks helping them. (Armstrong's journals)

First supply wagons arrive in Aspen

Prospectors could not live by silver and gold alone. They needed supplies, too. In isolated Aspen, it was big news on July 21, 1880, when savvy merchant H.P. Cowenhoven (right), his wife, Margaret, his daughter, Katherine, and his young clerk, D. R. C. Brown, pulled into town with two wagons full of supplies. Few could believe that they had negotiated formidable Taylor Pass above Ashcroft.

Rohrbough (1986) writes: "From a vantage point far above timberline, Cowenhoven and Brown looked down a slope so steep that the question was whether it was passable for men and horses, let alone wagons. Determined to take their cargo with them, they started down the impassable slope with two loaded wagons, but they measured progress in terms of yards, sometimes only a few hundred in the first days. On reaching the cliff edges, they unloaded the supplies, dissembled the wagons, and lowered them in sections by ropes and chains, pulleys and winches, to the next level ground below. There they reassembled the wagons, while Margaret and Katy Cowenhoven brought the mules, loaded with the goods by a more roundabout way to the new site. Then they reloaded the wagons and rehitched the mules . . . in two weeks they covered ten miles." (Lake County Public Library)

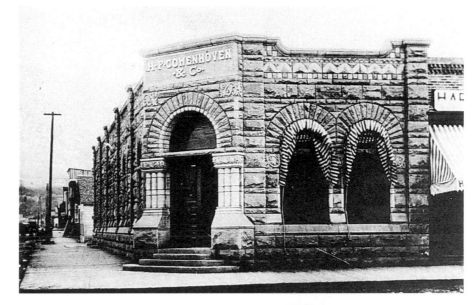

H. P. Cowenhoven & Co.

On July 22, 1880, "Grandpap" Cowenhoven, already 65 years old, purchased a corner lot at Cooper Avenue and Galena Street for $75. There he built the camp's fourth, and most impressive store. A later sandstone version (above) remains to this day. Within a few months Henry Gillespie's Roaring Fork Improvement Company completed a toll road over Taylor Pass, over which many more supply wagons easily rolled.

Cowenhoven's clerk, D. R. C. Brown, soon became his son-in-law. Brown went on to become a successful businessman, mine owner, and one of Aspen's major benefactors. Charles Armstrong, as indicated in his diaries (left), often shopped at Cowenhoven's store. (Lake Country Public Library) (Lake County Public Library) (Armstrong's journals)

Cowenhoven Tunnel

H. P. Cowenhoven also did well for himself during the next decade. One prominent mining publication (Canfield, 1893) wrote: "[Cowenhaven] arrived in Aspen in 1880, where he engaged in mercantile business, investing his profits in the mines as opportunity offered with such good judgment that he is now the largest owner of profitable mines in the entire district. He is now interested in the Aspen Mine, the Della S. Consolidated, the Deep Mining and Drainage Company, and any number of small properties. His investments extend into almost every branch of business, and he is now president of the Cowenhoven Mining, Drainage and Tunnel Company [above], the Roaring Fork Electric Light and Power Company, the Castle Creek Water Company, and vice-president of the First National Bank." (Lake County Public Library)

"Not a single bar of silver bullion"

*I*n 1883 Aspen, Independence, and Ashcroft all listed populations of 1,000. Thus, Aspen still found itself competing for prominence with neighboring camps. Several circumstances held back the Crystal City: the exorbitant expense of shipping ore to smelters in Leadville; no operable smelter; a labyrinth of mine-crippling litigation; no railroad; and a dearth of eastern capital. Even the extraction of ore (left, in a more recent photograph) lagged behind what everyone expected. Rohrbough (1986) notes: "In the spring of 1883, Aspen was four years old, and the occasion prompted no celebration. The camp had not produced a single bar of silver bullion. Aspen was a mining camp without mining". Yet with the arrival of a single man, Aspen's fortunes took a radical turn for the better. (Courtesy of Beck family collection)

33

Jerome B. Wheeler

*I*f ever a town had a real-life Santa Claus, Aspen came close with Jerome B. Wheeler. After serving with distinction in the Union Army in the Civil War, the astute Wheeler quickly became a successful businessman. In 1870 he married the niece of Randolph Macy, owner of New York's largest department store. By 1879 he earned a partnership in Macy's, but it was still not enough. A network of friendships led him to Aspen in 1883, where he determined that he could make his mark and an even larger fortune. (Able Breed's and David Hyman's initial investments sustained Aspen until Jerome Wheeler arrived.) Within two years Jerome purchased several mines, bought a partially constructed smelter, acquired coal mines in Crested Butte that produced hot-burning coke for the smelter, brought the first metallurgist (Walter B. Devereux) to Aspen to run the smelter, became partners with Gillespie in the Spar Mine, and opened Aspen's first bank — J. B. Wheeler and Company. As if these reputed $500,000 investments were not enough, in the late 1880s he helped finance Aspen's second railroad (the Colorado Midland), the elegant Wheeler Opera House, and the first-class Hotel Jerome. Almost single-handedly, Jerome B. Wheeler gave Aspen the financial momentum it needed to become one of the biggest and richest mining towns in Colorado. (Lake County Public Library)

1885 Aspen Directory
Introductory.

In presenting to the people of Aspen their first directory, I feel that my work is very inadequate to the needs of our beautiful and prosperous camp; but a first directory is always the most difficult; though owing to the liberal support of the merchants and the courtesy of all, I have been enabled to prepare this little volume, containing the names and address of about 800 permanent residents, which is a fair proportion out of a population of 3,000.

The prosperity of our little city, at the present time is wonderful. There are some 65 business houses in Aspen, using a combined capital aggregating over a half-million of dollars.

The mines, the basis our prosperity are producing well. The Spar, Washington, Vallejo, Emma and Aspen, situate on Aspen mountain, a half-mile south of the town; the Durant, Chloride and Camp Bird, on the same mountain a half-mile farther up, are the principal producers to the south of Aspen, though there are several other claims that have and are producing more or less mineral. To the north of town about a half-mile, on Smuggler hill, lies the Smuggler, and Smuggler 2, while there are some 25 or 30 good properties in the vicinity that only need development to make mines. The combined output of the mines is estimated at fully $500,000 per month. Thanks all for the kind and liberal patronage, I am yours truly,

J. C. DUFFY

Aspen, Jan. 1, 1885

First business directory

Without Jerome Wheeler, and some of his wealthy New York partners, this introduction to Aspen's first city business directory would not have been so positive.

Constructing a Log Cabin, Mason Elections, and a Promise

Wednesday, December 1, 1886. Pete and myself commenced work today. I am building a log cabin about 1 1/2 miles up Conundrum Gulch for assessment on the Eerie Placer claim. I am to get 16 dollars for it. Fine day.
Sunday, December 5, 1886. I finished the cabin yesterday. Have had splendid warm clear weather and I made good time. Built cabin 12 + 14 wide, 8 feet high, and split and put roof lagging on the roof and cut a door in.
Sunday, December 12, 1886. Fine morning, but cold. I went to Aspen Thursday evening to Mason's Election for year 87. Stopped all night. Ed Higenbothom kept house while I was gone. We bet each other a big supper that neither of us would take a drink of intoxicating beverage for one year from the 10th of Dec. 86. Aspen is very dull. All the topic is the great "Apex trial" at Denver. (Armstrong's journals)

Downtown Aspen

By the mid-1880s, it was clear that Aspen, not Independence or Ashcroft, would take center stage in the region. Shown here is downtown Aspen with Smuggler Mountain in the left background. Numerous carriages and coaches line dusty Cooper Avenue. All the buildings are wooden — a conflagration waiting to happen. A few business signs can be seen, including "Hooper Bros. Jewelers." (see opposite page). (Denver Public Library, Western History Department)

The Peru, Daubing the Cabin, Faro Bank, and a Rumor of a Strike

Saturday, January 1, 1887. New Years. Morning opened up clear and pleasant. I went up to the Milk Ranch and relocated the Peru, a claim that we did not do the assessment on last year. I went on the hill last Tuesday afternoon. Stopped in Besser's Cabin. Worked in our cabin Wednesday & Thursday. About finished it, except daubing. Came down in the evening. Snowed quite hard all day. Found the house full of bums. Pete and Tom Ogburn are packing grub up Conundrum. They are going to work up there all winter.

It is blowing & storming very hard this evening. I am alone with the dogs & cat. Schlag has gone back to town. He is no good. He is dead gone on Faro Bank. Blows in every cent he can get of his own, and mine too.

Saturday, January 8, 1887. I relocated two claims this year up near the "Milk Ranch." I hear that Robinson's have struck a good thing in the Dick Tunnel. If true, it will help us as we are on the same contact South of them. Things are looking brighter in this section than they have for some time. (Armstrong's journals)

37

Hooper Bros. Jewelers

This image exudes an aura of mining-town affluence. Over thirty well-dressed men stare at the camera from across Cooper Avenue. A shaggy dog reaches out his paw to one of the men near the door. Large watch advertisements hang from the telegraph pole on the corner. A piece of new furniture protrudes from the buggy by the front boardwalk. Barely visible behind the store is Aspen's distinctive wooden fire-bell tower. Hooper Brothers also sold musical instruments. (Colorado Historical Society, Stephen Hart Library)

HISTORIC ASPEN IN RARE PHOTOGRAPHS

38

Jack power

For years "jack trains" hauled ore over Independence Pass to Leadville. Once J. B. Wheeler's Aspen Mining and Smelter Works was "blown in," fewer jack trains had to make the expensive and arduous journey. Still, every day strings of mules and burrows hauled supplies to mines in the Aspen vicinity. By 1885 Aspenites pushed for another, more important form of transportation: "The great cry here now, is for the railroad. The nearest station is Crested Butte, 37 miles southwest; the next is Granite, 48 miles southeast, and next Leadville, 68 miles. Some of the young millionaires of the country, notably J. B. Wheeler & Co., are moving in the matter, but the route has not been decided upon" (Crofutt, 1885). (Courtesy of Adeline Zupancis Kirsten)

Fishing, An Aspen Ball, Feeling Lonesome, Jersey Lily, and July 4th

Friday, June 17, 1887. Very warm dry, weather. I was fishing a couple of hours this forenoon. Caught 6 trout, which made me a good meal at dinner. I am feeling rather lonesome this evening and kind of disgusted with this place. Have been here the most of 7 long years and have not made anything yet.

Friday, June 24, 1887. St Johns day. I ought to be in town today. The lodge turns out and marches in procession and winds up with a supper & Ball this evening. But, I don't feel able to spare the necessary Five Dollars. Schlag went to town Monday. Stayed till Thursday. Took $65.00 with him, which he spent, I suppose.

Monday, June 27, 1887. I was up to the Jersey Lily this forenoon, to see how she looked since Schlag did last year's assessment. Rainy day which I am glad to see. Baked bread today.

Tuesday, June 28, 1887. I went to town today by the stage. Spent $15.40. Only 90 cts for cigars. Got back at 3 oclock.

Monday, July 4, 1887. I went to Aspen today to see the celebration. It did not amount to much. The firemen had a parade and races by the different hose companies for prizes. That was all. (Armstrong's journals)

A SPAN OF ELK.

Elk power

A pair of trained elk turned heads in downtown Aspen. During the
1870s and 1880s prospectors and hunters depleted the elk herds
that roamed the Roaring Fork Valley. Decades later (see page 174),
Aspen imported elk on the railroad in an attempt to replenish the species.
(*Harper's Weekly*, January 19, 1889)

HISTORIC ASPEN IN RARE PHOTOGRAPHS

Packing Lumber, More Fish, Abe Lee, and a Bath in the Hot Springs

Sunday, July 24, 1887. Last Sunday night Schlag came back from town and went up to the Tunnel. Monday & Tuesday I packed lumber & mining timbers for John Boland on the Marion Mine. Wednesday I was at home. Went fishing for a short time. Caught 3 nice ones. Thursday packed a lot of stuff for Capt. Carey up to his camp. Friday I went up to Conundrum basin with Abe Lee [discovered gold in 1860 in California Gulch near present-day Leadville] *to hunt mountain sheep. Stayed till this morning. Did not see a sheep. But, had a couple of splendid baths in the hot springs. We have been having splendid weather for the last 4 or 5 days.* (Armstrong's journals)

"Kentucky Whiskies"

Aspen had its share of saloons, mostly along Cooper Avenue. B. T. Pearce & Co. advertised "Kentucky Whiskies," although the name on the wagon indicates Pearce sold spirits brewed in Denver as well. By 1889 over 35 saloons helped quench Aspen's considerable thirst. (Colorado Historical Society, Stephen Hart Library)

Men only

Saloons often served as meeting places for men. Respectable women did not frequent such places. Not only miners — notice the man with chaps — toasted the photographer in this scene. Brass spittoons are aligned under the foot-rail.

Vice in Aspen was taxed by the city at the monthly rate of "$25 each saloon, $10 for the first gaming table and $5 each additional table. And 'Sporting Women' were taxed at $5 per month" (Fredrick, 1999). (Aspen Historical Society)

Pierce's
MEMORANDUM
AND
ACCOUNT BOOK

designed for
Farmers, Mechanics
AND ALL PEOPLE

Who appreciate the value of keeping a memorandum of business transactions, daily events, and items of interest or importance, for future reference.

A PRESENT FROM THE
WORLD'S DISPENSARY MEDICAL ASSOCIATION

BUFFALO, N. Y., and LONDON, Eng.

According to Act of Congress, in the year 1884, by the "World's Dispensary Medical Association," in the office of the Librarian of Congress, at Washington.

1884.	APRIL.	1885.
S .. 6 13 20 27	THIS WILL REMIND ME OF	S .. 5 12 19 26
M .. 7 14 21 28	ARTICLES TO BE PUR-	M .. 6 13 20 27
T 1 8 15 22 29	CHASED.	T .. 7 14 21 28
W 2 9 16 23 30		W 1 8 15 22 29
T 3 10 17 24 ..		T 2 9 16 23 30
F 4 11 18 25 ..		F 3 10 17 24 ..
S 5 12 19 26 ..		S 4 11 18 25 ..

May 7th 1885

I do here by pledge myself not to drink anything intoxicating outside of our own bar or of our own liquor ~~or to smoke any cigars~~ and not more than 3 drinks a day there, and then only when not feeling well. for the space of 6 months from to day

Cha. S. Armstrong

9

Battling booze

Hangovers have caused many a person to swear off booze. On May 7, 1885, Charles S. Armstrong decided to curb his habit. His promise was as flimsy as the Pierce's Memorandum pamphlet in which he wrote it (left). Alcoholism, although not so identified then, took a terrible human toll in all Colorado mining towns. In 1885 Aspen's per day consumption of beer was 30 barrels in winter and 45 barrels in summer (Fredrick, 1999). (Armstrong's journals)

43

44

Clarendon Hotel

Since 1881, the three-story Clarendon Hotel on the corner of Durant Avenue and Mill Street (present-day Wagner Park) hosted guests and locals in thirty first-class rooms. This impressive wooden structure also served as one of Aspen's social centerpieces with its ladies parlor, ballroom, and upscale bar.

In November 1884, the storied Clarendon burned to the ground in two hours. The structure that took its place is shown above. Notice the wrap-around balcony outside the second floor. Three months earlier a fire leveled several downtown blocks and threatened to destroy the entire town. Something had to be done to improve the town's fire-fighting capabilities. (Courtesy of Adeline Zupancis Kirsten)

Picking Berries, Killing Grouse, Living High, and Doctoring

Thursday, August 23, 1887. Schlag quit work on the tunnel the 8th and went to Aspen. Came back on the 20th and went up Conundrum to work on the Jersey Lilly. Ed Higenbothom is with him. Ed stopped with me here week before last. We had a fine time picking berries and Ed killed 5 nice grouse and I caught plenty of trout, so we lived high. I was up and measured the tunnel Sunday. It is 164 feet, but shows a little galena through the lime. I was up on the hill yesterday. Examined the Rif. The water is below the drift. Will have to fix it up some as it has caved some. Wm Oliphant is boarding. Has been here a week. He is sick and is laying up and doctoring. (Armstrong's journals)

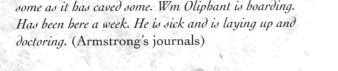

Fire protection

After the Clarendon burned, concerned citizens quickly formed a volunteer fire hose company. In 1885, the same year that the new Clarendon reopened, Aspen spent $3,000 to have fireplugs installed and connected to the privately owned (by D. R. C. Brown and H. P. Cowenhoven) Aspen Water Company's ditches. In 1886, Mr. and Mrs. Henry Gillespie purchased a 2,000 pound fire bell for the city. It can still be seen today outside the Aspen Fire Department building on Hopkins Avenue.

By 1889 the Aspen City Directory listed Hose Company No. 1, Cowenhoven Hose No. 2, Red Star Hose Company No. 3, and the J. D. Hooper Hook and Ladder Company (shown above). Later, ordinances requiring downtown structures to be brick or stone significantly reduced the danger of a conflagration. Yet neither fire ordinances nor improved fire-fighting equipment kept the bell tower from becoming a smoldering heap of ashes many years later, after being abandoned. (Aspen Historical Society)

45

46

Winter fire wagon

*T*he Aspen Fire Department rigged this small hook and ladder wagon for winter duty. At the rear of the wagon two fire department members pose in full fire-fighting gear with a spiked fire axe and pipe (long hose nozzle). From the middle of the wagon a young boy peers at the camera. At the feet of the driver is a large shiny bell. The driver rang the bell by stomping on a foot-pedal device attached to the bell's ringer. (University of Wyoming, American Heritage Center)

Knights of Pythias

Early Aspen City Directories listed them as "SECRET AND BENEVOLENT SOCIETIES." Members of the Aspen Masons, Odd Fellows, Grand Army of the Republic, Knights of Pythias, Knights of Honor, and Good Templars took their club membership and vows seriously. Posing in military-like regalia seemed to be part of the appeal as well. These social fraternities covered burial costs for their members and cared for widows and orphans of members who died. The proliferation of such organizations reflected the dangers of mining. Most such organizations also conscientiously supported worthwhile community causes.

Here, the Knights of Pythias, Leadville Lodge, No. 1, pose during a visit to the Crystal City. Mustaches seem to be the order of the day. A young boy sits in front with a snare drum. Two African-Americans, one holding a rooster, flank the three men sitting cross-legged in the first row. (Denver Public Library, Western History Department)

47

The winter social season

Annual winter galas and masquerade balls sponsored by various secret and benevolent societies proved to be the highlights of the winter social season well into the twentieth century. (Both from Museum of Western Colorado)

48

"Aspen Volunteers"

No social club, this assembly of men called themselves the "Aspen Volunteers." In 1887 three of them died during a skirmish with a group of Utes who had "fled the reservation" in Utah Territory. During this era, no love was lost for Utes or anyone sympathetic to their cause. (Aspen Historical Society)

49

News of the War Scare

Thursday, August 23, 1887 . . . The Utes have got up a war scare over at Meeker, and the state is sending the militia over there. The Aspen company went over there last week. And Sheriff Hooper, with 45 men, volunteered and have gone to fight the Utes too. I got a letter from home last week. The folks are all well. I have put up a nice lot of red raspberry jelly & jam the past week.
Sunday, August 28, 1887 . . . The news from the Ute war is [that] a battle [was] fought on Thursday. Three whites killed & 7 wounded. One of the dead is from Aspen — Lieutenant of the Aspen militia, Folsome by name. Also one of wounded is from Aspen. Three Utes killed & some hurt. (Armstrong's journals)

50

School time

*I*n September 1881, Aspen's first school opened with an enrollment of ten boys and fourteen girls. Later in the year the enrollment jumped to fifty-three. By 1885 school age children numbered 302, but only 175 were enrolled. Construction had already begun on a second school in east Aspen. Yet another school, Lincoln (center), served the Crystal City in the late nineteenth and early twentieth century.

Students (above) in an Aspen elementary school sit at wooden desks. The girls wear dresses with puffed sleeves and high collars; boys wear long-sleeved shirts, jackets, and trousers. A centrally located cast iron stove heated the classroom during winter. Categories listed on an Aspen Public School report card (right) indicate a traditional approach to education. Punctuality and deportment were also evaluated. (Both from Denver Public Library, Western History Department) (Report card: Museum of Western Colorado)

52

The Aspen Times

O n April 23, 1881, occupants of the small camp welcomed the first issue of their first newspaper: *The Aspen Times*. B. Clark Wheeler started and owned the newspaper. The editor declared, "A NEWSPAPER in a rich and growing mining camp like Aspen, is more than an advantage; it is a necessity. That necessity is two-fold, for the newspaper in a mining camp assumes two duties, the one being to furnish the camp with the news of the outside world, and the other to furnish the outside world with a knowledge of the production and of the strikes in the camp."

Later, in this image *The Aspen Daily Times* plant crew (twelve men, one woman) stand on the wood-plank sidewalk in front of the *Times* office on Cooper Avenue. This photograph was probably taken in the late 1890s. Before the end of the decade, *The Aspen Daily Chronicle* and the *Rocky Mountain Sun* competed with the *Times*. (Masthead courtesy of Ben Kirsten) (Denver Public Library, Western History Department)

53

From on high

Although they already lived in a lofty alpine valley, Aspenites sought even higher spiritual guidance. Unassuming Christ Church and rectory (above), shown here in 1887, ministered to this need. By 1890 the impressive brick First Presbyterian Church (right) on the corner of Bleeker and Aspen sought to save even more souls. (Denver Public Library, Western History Department) (Courtesy of Adeline Zupancis Kirsten)

HISTORIC ASPEN IN RARE PHOTOGRAPHS

54

Inside St. Mary's Catholic Church

Father Edward Downey and three alter boys pose in their vestments in front of the altar in St. Mary's Catholic Church in 1885. Pews are in the foreground. Two chandeliers with glass globes hang from the ceiling. Garlands of small flowers adorn the altar. The stations of the cross are visible next to the windows on the side walls. By 1889, Aspenites had a choice of six different denominational houses of worship. (Denver Public Library, Western History Department)

A Lunar Rainbow, A Bear, the Little Annie, and Plentiful Grapes

September, 1, 1887. Fine fall day. Cap Carey and all the hands went to Aspen this morning. Foggy day. Night before last I saw a Lunar Rainbow. The first I ever saw. It was raining down the gulch and the moon was shining in the east and made a clear, distinct rainbow in the North West. I saw a bear day before yesterday at noon on the hillside opposite the house. I & Wm. Oliphant went after him, but he saw us and skipped out. We could not find him again.

Saturday, September 17, 1887 . . . I got up at 5:30 this morning. Wm. Oliphant left this morning. Has gone to work on the Little Annie at running the hoister. For the last two days, I have been picking and making jelly of Oregon [?] Grapes. They are very plentiful. The hillside opposite the house is blue with them. Schlag is with Abe Lee up in Conundrum Basin. I commenced cutting the oats today. They are nicely headed and will make fine feed, if I can cure them good. (Armstrong's journals)

Mill Street

*L*ooking north down Mill Street, this stereoview shows the second Clarendon Hotel (far left with balcony), first courthouse (white, beneath Clarendon sign), the Wheeler Opera House (tall brick building with arched windows) and the Hotel Jerome (two-story brick building at the end of the street). Telephone poles tower over Mill Street. Their crossarms carried rows of glass insulators, some of them manufactured in Denver (inset). Facing the camera is a small girl on a donkey. She posed for other stereoviews (see pages 78-79) as well, mostly in the 1890s and early 1900s. (University of Wyoming, American Heritage Center) (Author's collection)

5573. Aspen, Col. U. S, A.

55

56

"Incandescent purity of electric lights"

On May 23, 1885, *The Aspen Daily Times* reported: "The Aspen Electric Company last evening turned on the friction, and forty places of business were instantly aglow with an incandescent purity of electric lights. The motive power is furnished by the immense water power plant of the Aspen Smelter. For the young city of Aspen this is a great achievement." An interior view of the electric power plant is shown above. Notice the two large generators with belts resting on wood bases, and the electrical boxes and other circuitry on the back wall. On the back of the photograph someone wrote: "Built in 1885 — one of first hydro-electric plants in the United States producing direct current." (Denver Public Library, Western History Department)

A Pugilist Exhibition, Snow, Old Jerry, and Assessment Work

Wednesday, November 23, 1887. I went to Aspen yesterday afternoon settled with Cap. Carey. Had to allow him $7.40 on the work on the tunnel, but he says he will never ask us to put up again till he can take the pay out of the mine. Cap. goes to Denver on the 9.55 train today. I stayed in town all night. Went to [see] McHenry Johnson, [at] the colored pugilist exhibition. It was pretty good. After that was out, took in all the sights of the town till daylight. Got home today at noon. Snowed all last night and today and still is snowing.

Thursday, December 1, 1887. I have been getting up wood for the house today, used Old Jerry to pack it. I went on to the hill a week ago today to finish assessment work on the Phoenix. About a foot of snow fell Thursday & Friday and the weather was very cold. (Armstrong's journals)

HALLAM LAKE.

Hallam Lake

In 1889 an illustrator for a popular nationwide magazine drew this scene and wrote these words: "On the lake the stroller may see the splash of oars in the moonlight, and hear the hum of voices from some idling boat, while high overhead, on the precipitous front of Aspen Mountain, shine the lights from the mines, so far away, and yet so bright, that they look like stars" (*Harper's Weekly,* January 19, 1889).

Aspen's dance pavilion reflects off Hallam Lake, a popular recreational area for young and old citizens. Galas, pleasure-boating, ice-skating, and even a flume ride kept people coming to this picturesque spot throughout the year. Novice gala attendees could learn the "Polite Art of Dancing" at G. A. Godat's Dancing Academy (right). (Aspen City Directory, 1893)

58

Historic Aspen in Rare Photographs

Leadville, Colo *Sept 7* *1881.*

M. Manvill & Mc

To **WALL & WITTER,** *Dr*

LIVERY, FEED AND SALE STABLE.

PROPRIETORS OF

Twin Lakes, Independence and Aspen Stage Line.

FINEST STOCK AND ELEGANT CARRIAGES.

Aspen's lifeblood since 1880

In the early 1880s Aspen needed transportation to survive. Soon toll roads, toll bridges, and stage lines fulfilled that need. Mule trains and freight wagons hauled ore to smelters over these rough, high routes. Stage lines hauled Aspenites, cargo, and mail (bottom right) back and forth to railroad and mining hubs. As for stage passengers, rocky roads and rough receptions (far left) made for many memorable journeys.

One of the earliest stages to Aspen followed much of the same trail over Independence Pass that Charles Armstrong negotiated in May 1880. By 1881 Leadville's Wall and Witter (top right) ran the "Twin Lakes, Independence, and Aspen Stage Line" with the "finest stock and elegant carriages". (*Frank Leslie's Illustrated Newspaper,* November 11, 1882) (Author's collection) (Courtesy of Gary Bracken)

59

Railroads meant everything

By 1887, as the Denver and Rio Grande and the Colorado Midland Railway crews frantically pushed their lines toward Aspen, several stage line companies watched their sure demise progress. Of course, Aspen citizens counted the days until the first engine finally chugged into their silver fields. Railroads meant everything to remote mining towns like Aspen. Immediately, more low-grade ore could be shipped at less expense to Leadville, Denver, and beyond. Overnight, a cornucopia of reasonably priced supplies tempted townspeople. And within weeks, more people, more money, more business, and more prestige rolled into the heart of the Crystal City.

Left, a Colorado Midland work crew poses for a photographer on top of the great 1,084-foot-long timber trestle above Busk Creek on the east side of Hagerman Pass. Once finished, the Colorado Midland line would connect Aspen to Leadville. Meanwhile, Denver and Rio Grande construction workers raced toward Aspen from Glenwood Springs through the more receptive topography of the Roaring Fork Valley. (Denver Public Library, Western History Department)

A Ride on the Construction Train and Fine Weather

Wednesday, October 26, 1887. I walked to Aspen this forenoon. Walked down to see the R.R. with Fred Bassager. It is about 2 1/2 miles below town. Had a ride on the construction train about 1/4 of a mile. The first ride, and the first train of cars, that I have been on since March 1881. They are laying about 3 miles per day. The gauge is narrow, but the ties are long enough for another rail which they propose to shortly . . . [make] . . . Standard gauge. The first engine which will be into Aspen is No 82. This is fine weather for all kinds of work out of doors. I had the plow fixed and bought some goods and sent them home by Tom Morris of the Tenderfoot. (Armstrong's journals)

Loops to the top

Colorado Midland's tracks ascend the east slope of Hagerman Pass (left). The main line from Leadville climbs along the southeast side of the valley. A majestic trestle, an amazing feat of engineering at nearly 11,000 feet in elevation, rises in the right foreground. Four railroad loops wind around high canyons. The buildings near the track are part of raucous Douglas City, a construction camp for mostly Italian laborers. In 1893, a famed 2,164-foot tunnel diverted rail traffic under the trestle and the Continental Divide. (Denver Public Library, Western History Collection)

61

A Variety Show, The Railroad Arrives, Fair Sleighing, and a Deadly Snow Slide

Thursday, October 27, 1887. *I stayed in Aspen last night with Sam Selden. We attended the Variety Show & c [etc.]. The R..R.. got into Aspen this evening. The town people are going to treat the hands with a Barbecue & grand blow out.*

Thursday, December 1, 1887. *I saw the Midland R..R.. for the first time Monday, looking from park on the hill. I finished work Tuesday afternoon and came down home yesterday. I hunted up the jacks and packed the bedding & c. off the hill. Very fair sleighing to town. Cap. Carey & men quit work and came down the gulch late Friday. That finishes work on the Grand Union for this year. Fogg took down the bodies of Culver & Wilson that were killed in a snow slide up Pine Creek above Ashcroft last month. The bodies were found last week. Schlag quit work on the Puzzler a week ago. The Midland R..R.. has finished the bridge over Maroon and are running into Aspen.*
(Armstrong's journals)

"Kit Carson's" last staging into Aspen?

This view of the last stagecoach run from Emma, Pitkin County, Colorado, shows a crowd by, according to the archival description on the photograph, "Kit Carson's" stagecoaches and horse-drawn wagons, a balloon-stacked engine, and freight car of the Denver and Rio Grande Railroad. That Kit Carson died in 1868 suggests his connection to this stage company was in name only. (Denver Public Library, Western History Department)

First the Denver and Rio Grande

O n October 27, 1887, track layers with the Denver and Rio Grande Railroad construction crew reached Aspen. Within a week the first "official train" arrived and the Denver and Rio Grande depot opened for business on 331 East Hyman Avenue. Ecstatic citizens (above) gathered to welcome the first locomotive to rumble into Aspen. (Denver Public Library, Western History Department)

Dignitaries and a $5,000 celebration

A tumultuous week-long celebration greeted the first Denver and Rio Grande train in early November 1887. Many dignitaries road the rails to town, including Henry M. Teller (right), Colorado's first senator, foremost silver advocate, and mining lawyer extraordinaire. A few years earlier, Teller played a major role in settling Aspen's pivotal and protracted "apex litigation." Aspen Mine owners (called "sideliners") found themselves pitted against the Durant Mine owners (called "apexers"). Durant Mine owners asserted that if the apex of a vein on their claim broke the surface, that they had a right to follow it wherever it might lead — including through other legal claims. For years sideliners had prevailed. It only made sense, thought most of the mining world. Then, to the everlasting astonishment of Aspen Mine owners, in 1886 a jury sided (no pun intended) with the apexers. Intelligent and forceful Teller was able to work out a compromise between the two parties, but hard feelings lasted for decades, and mining law took a radical twist.

Toward the end of the century, the newly formed Silver Party wanted Henry Teller to carry its presidential banner. Later, Teller's son Harrison used his 1912 complimentary railroad pass (below) to travel to Aspen. (Both from author's collection)

64

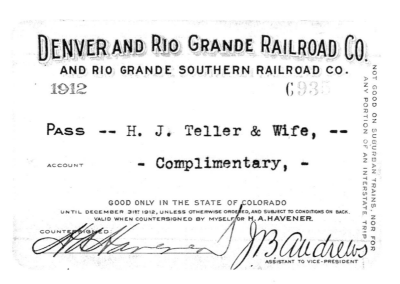

Here comes the Midland

A stunning Colorado Midland broadside (left) discovered within the walls of an old home in Leadville solicited passengers to ride one of the first Colorado Midland trains into the "Mouth of the Frying Pan." (Courtesy of Gary Bracken)

Maroon bridge on the Midland Railway to Aspen

After clearing the Continental Divide, bridging the steep-banked Castle Creek and Maroon Creek cost the Colorado Midland precious time. Finally, the Midland's depot on the corner of Durant Avenue and Hunter Street opened for business in February 1888. This second railroad line solidified Aspen's reputation as one of the brightest mining spots in the nation.

In 1889 an artist penned an indelible image (right) of a Colorado Midland train puffing across the dramatic metal bridge — 650 feet in length — erected over Maroon Creek. Of his trip to Aspen a passenger observed: "The traveler no longer climbs the Continental Divide in a jolting coach and six or a laboring freight wagon, but takes his case in a Pullman palace-car; and sees in the streets of Aspen buildings of brick and stone instead of log huts and wall tents" (*Harper's Weekly*, January 19, 1889). (*Harper's Weekly*, January 19, 1889)

66

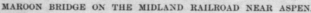
MAROON BRIDGE ON THE MIDLAND RAILROAD NEAR ASPEN.

Over the rails they came

O n April 2, 1888, in Leadville, Colorado, Swede Henry Beck became a citizen of the United States of America. Within a few years he married and road the rails to Aspen. Like other hard-working immigrants, he soon rose to prominence in Aspen. The dedicated family man (left) and successful business entrepreneur became a state legislator in the early twentieth century.

In 1908, ten-year-old Carl Gustaf Beck (far right, sitting in his mother's lap) wrote an essay about his town (see next page). During this era it was common to dress young boys in feminine clothes. (Courtesy of the Beck family collection)

67

Our Town

Carl Gustaf Beck
1908

It is a small mining town. Its altitude is seven thousand, seven hundred and seventy nine feet. It is called Aspen. If it were not for the mines of Aspen, Aspen would not be what it is. The Mollie Gibson and the Smuggler Mines are the most important. They were once upon a time the second to the richest in the world. There are many other mines in Aspen.

The people that first came to Aspen made their way over the Independence mountain. The people came and the population in twenty five years was three thousand. Now days, two railroads run from Aspen to Denver. The Midland is one of the trains and the Denver Rio Grande is the other.

Aspen is the prettiest mining camp in the United States. It has the nicest Opera house of any mining camp. It also has stores of all kinds. Aspen has many schools.

Aspen has four rivers. Castle creek separates the town from the country. Maroon is a river with lots of log jams in it. Roaring Fork and Hunter Creek are muddy. They both run mills. Above the mill, Roaring Fork is clear and still.

(Courtesy of the Beck family collection)

Henry Beck's whiskey jugs and soda pop bottles

Near the turn of the century Beck became the sole proprietor of a successful wholesale liquor and cigar business and the old Aspen Bottling Works — signified by the "ABW" embossed on its bottles (left). Beck's whiskey came in jugs (far left) and his soda pop came in dated bottles. They both helped quench citizens' thirst. (Courtesy of Rick Sinner) (Courtesy of Ralph Kemper)

69

Behaving Badly

Saturday, June 9, 1888. I went to Aspen this morning. Walked down. Stayed in town all day. Nothing going on. I drank considerable beer more than I needed, but not enough to get off. *Sunday June 10th 1888. I stayed in Aspen all night. Did not go to bed at all. Went to the show and it was about 1 oclock when it let out, so I set up till daylight. Took several cocktails in the morning which did me no good. So I first came to the conclusion to not touch any intoxicating drinks for a year from today. I walked up home this forenoon. Got home about noon. Very warm day. Have not felt good all day — the evil effects of beer and getting no sleep all night. (Armstrong's journals)*

Mining ruled

*A*spen owed its very existence to the mines. This bird's-eye view of north Aspen includes numerous mines and businesses at the base of Aspen Mountain. Starting from left center small numbers — some a challenge to spot — identify the Colorado Midland depot (23), Aspen Public Tramway (25) — one mile long with 86 buckets, Durant Mining Company's Tramway and Ore House (27), Taylor and Brunton Sampling Works (50), Aspen Mine Tramway and Ore House (28), and Durant Tunnel (30). Center right is the Aspen Deep Mining and Drainage Company (31), Enterprise Mine (32), and the Aspen Mining and Smelting Company — including the Veteran Tunnel (33). Upper left is Garfield School with the number four on its roof (4), Finley and Rose Lumber Yard (60), and the Aspen Smelting Company (81). Upper right is a portion of the Evergreen Cemetery (34). (Courtesy of Ben Kirsten)

Assayers

Mine owners and managers depended heavily on assayers. Reliable and trustworthy assayers could earn a good living. Aspen photographer D. R. Drenkel snapped this rare view of the interior of a local assayer's laboratory. A balance scale, chemical bottles, glass beakers, and a large exhaust fan in a tidy room bespeak a preciseness necessary for high-quality assay work. (Courtesy of George Foott)

71

Architectural and social symbols of success

I n 1889 everything seemed new in Aspen. The newly opened Wheeler Opera House (right) made a grand architectural and civic statement about Aspen's arrival as a center for the performing arts. "The building is thoroughly heated with steam and lighted by electricity. There are to be, when finished, over 300 electric lights" (*Rocky Mountain Sun,* November 30, 1889).

Equally new, the three-story luxuriant Hotel Jerome (opposite page) served as an anchor for the Crystal City's twenty city blocks. "Connected with the hotel is a large greenhouse, in which are raised the vegetables and various products practicable in such a place for the use of the table of the hotel, it can place before its guests better than the market affords for many months of the year" (Canfield, 1893).

Both of these edifices served as symbols of Aspen's soaring success. It seemed that nothing could stop the Crystal City from taking its place as one of the best and most prosperous cities in the West, let alone Colorado. (Both courtesy of Adeline Zupancis Kirsten)

72

On Being Foolish, B. Clark Wheeler, and the Death of a Noble Man

Saturday, September 7, 1889. Feeling pretty good considering I spent foolishly for drinks &c., $7.50 cash money that I needed. It seems though that I never will learn anything.

Tuesday, September 10, 1889. Schlag packed up a load for B. Clark Wheeler today and brought down a load of ore for the Little Annie mine. I have been around the house all the week cutting grass and loafing. Washed my clothes today.

Sunday, October 13, 1889. The Little Annie is working in [a] good shaft and will make a mine without doubt. Everybody on the hill is feeling good over the prospects.

Thursday, December 5, 1889. Sad news to me today. L. J. W. Vary, one of nature's noble men, died this morning about 7 oclock of heart disease. He was elected county Treasurer this fall, but did not live long enough to go into office. He is an old timer in the camp and has rustled with the rest of us. I don't see where they will find a man to fill his place. (Armstrong's journals)

74

"Aspen is to be congratulated"

With glistening new buildings, rich mines, two railroads, scenic environs, and a population pushing 10,000, the Crystal City's 1889 City Directory patted itself on the back: "Aspen is to be congratulated on the prominence she has attained." The nation's most popular illustrated magazine, *Harper's Weekly*, featured the Crystal City in January 1889. Railroad tourist books also touted Aspen's assets: "Stores and shops of all kinds, carrying large lines of goods, are abundant, and the business done here would do credit to a town boasting five times its present population . . . . It is a town of beautiful homes, and has most excellent society . . . . The climate is delicious and especially beneficial in all pulmonary complaints. Aspen is a garden town, and displays many beautiful lawns, sprinkled and beautified by flowers . . . . The main industry is mining . . . . The ores are of good grade and are found in remarkably large deposits" (Wood, 1889).

A more promising future could not be asked for by any mountain mining town. (*Harper's Weekly*, January 19, 1889)

HISTORIC ASPEN IN RARE PHOTOGRAPHS

CHAPTER TWO
Boom and Bust (1890s)

During the early 1890s Aspen boomed on the backs of fabulously rich silver mines, like the Mollie Gibson and Smuggler. In 1892 the Crystal City even outshone its big brother, Leadville, by producing over $10,000,000 in silver, one-sixth of the nation's supply. Now the third largest city in Colorado (behind Denver and Leadville), Aspen acted like it. Its citizens had their choice of four newspapers, three banks, two railroads, two opera houses, thirteen physicians, twenty-one attorneys, twenty-seven saloons, eight churches, thirty-five secret and benevolent societies, and two cemeteries. A state-of-the-art hook and ladder company and three fire hose companies stood ready to douse any fire that threatened to reduce Aspen to ashes. Demanding schools pointed young lives in proper directions. A modern, hygienic hospital ministered to the needs of the injured and sick. An impressive courthouse and stout jail served as constant visual reminders that the law would be obeyed. Public, horse-drawn trolleys made travel from one end of the city to the other safe and convenient. Stimulating cultural events edified upper class citizens' minds, while theatrical productions, galas, and costume parties filled their social calendars. Avid fans flocked to see crucial baseball games against Leadville and Ashcroft. Boating in the summer and ice skating in the winter could be enjoyed by all on lovely Hallam Lake just north of town. Even the noxious smelter smoke hanging over the city signaled that the town's money machines — the silver mines — thrived.

Downtown, businesses flourished. Astute brokers sold customers high-quality mining stocks. Drugstores and pharmacies carried their own brands of cures in customized bottles. Bookstores stocked popular novels, weekly magazines, a wide array of office supplies, and leather-bound journals. Clothing stores displayed the latest in fashions. Hardware shelves groaned under the weight of mining and maintenance supplies. Blacksmiths and wagon makers wore out tools trying to keep up with demands. Photographers competed for the lucrative portrait and landscape trade. Laundries scrambled to keep up with cleaning needs. New businesses opened almost daily. Land prices soared. Small wonder train excursionists left Aspen believing that Aspen would soon become "Denver west of the Continental Divide."

Maybe such runaway success kept Aspenites from thinking about the financial disaster that loomed so close. On a more basic psychological plane, maybe people could not seriously entertain the possibility of an abrupt halt to such heady prosperity. Yet all the signs were clearly there. Everyone knew that for years the United States government had been purchasing silver at inflated prices because of the Sherman Silver Purchase Act. Everyone also knew that powerful forces back east wanted this practice stopped. Even the president of the United States wanted gold to back our currency, not silver and gold. Yet, for whatever reasons, silver-mining towns in Colorado, including booming Aspen, chose not to take this monetary issue seriously.

By the time Aspen saw the gold standard coming, it was too late. During the early 1890s, Colorado politicians did what they could to defeat the powerful eastern "goldbugs," who wanted this "demonic gold-backed monetary system." However, there was probably nothing Coloradans could have done about it. The general economy of the United States was already in the doldrums, and with the steadily declining price of silver on the world market, several of Britain's silver mints in India closed on June 26, 1893. More nations throughout the

world were turning to gold, rather than silver, to back their currency. Even the entire West did not have enough clout in Congress to keep the government buying silver at inflated prices to buoy the bimetallic (silver and gold) monetary system. Suddenly, during that fateful July in 1893 when the United States finally repealed the Sherman Silver Purchase Act, the bottom fell out of the price of silver — dropping it to about 60 cents an ounce, less than one-half its value in 1879. Within weeks most silver mines in the Aspen region closed, crippling the economy of Aspen. The first boom was over. Aspen would have to wait for over a half-century for another.

The collapse of silver prices in the early 1890s strikes most people as nothing more than a bit of uninteresting historical fiscal policy. But consider the implications. In a matter of days in 1893, a change in the United States government's "uninteresting" monetary policy led to the demise of many great silver mining centers, including Aspen and Leadville — both of which had been the envy of the world. Even today few people understand that our specie [coins] and paper currency are no longer backed by either silver or gold. Rather, our money has value only in that people are willing to accept it for goods and services. Should people suddenly decide not to accept our money, because it cannot be exchanged for either silver or gold, it could become worthless overnight.

Because of the calamitous monetary events, by the end of the summer of 1893, fewer than fifteen percent of Aspen's work force was employed. A trickle of people leaving the Crystal City to seek employment elsewhere increased to a steady stream during the fall of 1893. In 1894, when the price of silver climbed slightly, a few mines reopened. A brief period of optimism resulted. Then just as things started to level off in the summer of 1896, a wave of discontent swept through the overworked and underpaid miners. For years the miners' unions in Colorado had accepted lower wages and poor benefits (if any), to keep the mines operating. Although violence never erupted in Aspen as it did in Leadville, where near-anarchy prevailed, it simmered close enough to the surface to make everyone extremely uncomfortable.

From the past, Charles Armstrong speaks to us about these events. Historians necessarily speak in generalities, "boom and bust," "fiscal policies," and "crippling unemployment." Armstrong personalizes these generalities. In other words, Armstrong — although at times maddeningly mundane — puts a human face on Aspen's boom and bust decade.

Armstrong left us another personal perspective as well. As mentioned before, he drew. At times I am tempted to call it doodling, but it was more than that. Examine the mosaic of impressions on the last page (see page 135) of this chapter which he penned on the inside of the back cover of his 1897 - 1899 journal. It captures one of the last significant international events of the nineteenth century: the sinking of the *Maine*. I can envision him at night in his log cabin beside Castle Creek. Light from the thin glass globe of his kerosine lantern flickers through the crude glass windows. Inside, Armstrong leans over his journal on the handmade table with his ink pen in hand. Nearby sits a half empty inkwell. He is thinking about Aspen. He is thinking about the rise and fall of the nation's fortunes. He wonders about the sinking of the *Maine* and war with Spain. He starts to draw. Soon his thoughts become pictures.

77

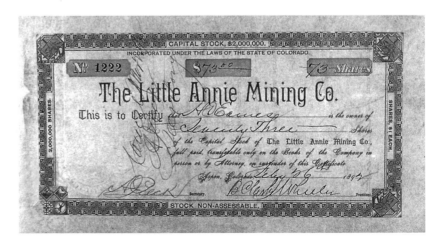

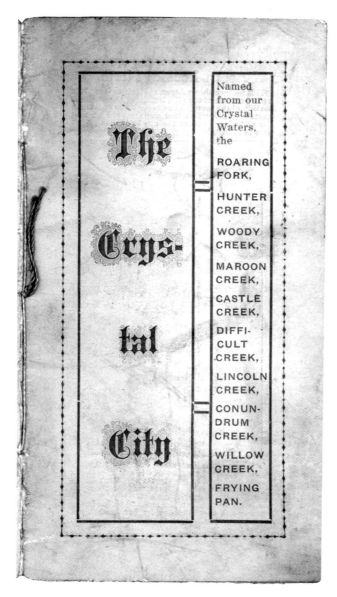

The Crys-tal City

Named from our Crystal Waters, the

ROARING FORK,

HUNTER CREEK,

WOODY CREEK,

MAROON CREEK,

CASTLE CREEK,

DIFFI-CULT CREEK,

LINCOLN CREEK,

CONUN-DRUM CREEK,

WILLOW CREEK,

FRYING PAN.

JAMES M. DAVIS,
New York, St. Louis, Liverpool Toronto, Sydney.

5577.

Copyright 1890, by B. W. Kilburn.

e frightened, old Jenny is true, Aspen, Col., U. S. A.

"Aspen out-rivals Aladdin and Monte Cristo"

A cover (far left) of a small pamphlet printed by the Aspen Commercial Club (apparently in the early 1890s) lists the "Crystal Waters" that gave Aspen its nickname. In 1893 a book featuring Colorado mines and mining men wrote of the Crystal City: "There are men to-day who count their riches by the hundreds of thousands, whose hands have been familiar with the pick, shovel and hammer, and whose daily toll barely sufficed to provide a meagre supply of life's necessities. The history of Aspen is instructive because it teaches the value of pluck and perseverance; it is romantic because the result has out-rivaled the fabled achievements of Aladdin or a Monte Cristo" (Canfield, 1893).

Two children on a burro and a man holding the reigns pose for the photographer (left) on the west side of the Little Nell. Fabled Aspen stretches out behind them. The Clarendon Hotel, Wheeler Opera House, and the Hotel Jerome line the west (left) side of Mill Street. Aspen's distinctive wooden fire-bell tower can be seen opposite the Clarendon Hotel. (Both from author's collection)

79

First National Bank

While the crystal waters flowed, money gushed in downtown Aspen. Shown here is Aspen's First National Bank on the corner of Galena Street and Hopkins Avenue. Aspen National Bank and J. B. Wheeler & Company Bank also catered to the Crystal City's considerable financial needs. (Lake County Public Library)

80

Deadly Mines, Throwing Rock, Overturned Stage, and an Accident

Friday, February, 14, 1890. Malon Hamaker was killed in the Aspen mine yesterday by falling down a shaft. There was a man killed day before and this morning. And hear one met his fate on Aspen Mountain. Accidents seem to go by threes.

Thursday, April 17, 1890. Fine day. I put in the most of the day working on the road throwing out rock &c. Frogg upset the stage near the bridge this side of Lime Gulch, and I helped him get righted up.

Saturday, August 28, 1890. John Coll, Fred Bassager, and myself, went to Crested Butte this morning. And while we were gone, Mike Coleman blowed his right hand off with a giant Cartridge while trying to blow up a woodchuck hole. (Armstrong's journals)

Pitkin County Courthouse

Prominent Denver architect William Quayle designed this imposing structure that anchors east Main Street to this day. Ironically, during the construction of the courthouse in the late 1880s, *The Aspen Daily Times* accused the county commissioners of financial irregularities. No wrong doing ever surfaced and the courthouse was finally completed in 1891. (Courtesy of Adeline Zupancis Kirsten)

81

Strike up the band

Aspen had every reason to strike up the band in the early 1890s. Its population had soared to over 12,000. Aspen's silver production even surpassed its big brother, Leadville, to the tune of $10,000,000 annually. Now the third largest city in the state, the Crystal City seemed destined for greatness.

Above, uniformed members of a brass band march down a dirt Cooper Avenue during a parade. A man on a bicycle and two pedestrians watch the spectacle. Two children hold the hands of a woman as they walk down the sidewalk. The signs on the buildings read: "The Silver Club," "Liquor," "Produce," "Lewis H. Tomkins," and "Lion Coffee." (Denver Public Library, Western History Department)

Aspen Drum Corp

*T*he elite Aspen Drum Corp entertained appreciative locals on special holidays and at important social functions. They also competed successfully with other drum corps throughout the state. (University of Wyoming, American Heritage Center)

On Being a Fool, The Clarendon, and Big Guns of the Railroad

Friday, April 7, 1891. Came home this afternoon, after making as big a fool of myself as possible.

Sunday, May 31, 1891. Lodged at the Clarendon last night. Was at the hose ball game today.

Friday, June 26, 1891. Washed some clothes today. Got lunch at noon, for about 15 Big Guns of the Midland R.R., that Charlie Franklin and Jess Waters were taking up on Richmond Hill to look at the Park & Mamie [?] Mine. The secretary of state of Colo. was amongst them. They were a nice sociable lot of men. Was talking with Maj. Pickrel this evening. He has got to work on the Grand Union in good shape. (Armstrong's journals)

84

"Opie & Kerr Portraits and Views"

*A*spen photographers captured many wonderful historic images. This photograph shows five local ladies in old-world European attire. Only the 1891 Aspen City Directory listed "Opie & Kerr Portraits and Views." (Courtesy of Bruce and Hillary McCallister)

Selective open arms

Not all ethnic groups were welcomed with open arms. Aspen, as most frontier mining towns, found itself partitioned into ethnic enclaves. Irish, German, Slovenian, Austrian, and Italian immigrants populated the East End. Swedish immigrants settled in Oklahoma Flats or the Dean Addition. Wealthier Protestant entrepreneurs lived in the West End. People of Chinese, African, and American-Indian descent were seldom welcomed with open arms.

Even toys reflected the prejudice of the era. The top gun shows a man pulling down a derby over an Italian's ears. On the right a Chinese person gets his queue (a long strang of braided hair) jerked (the queue part is missing) while simultaneously getting the boot. (Both courtesy of Ed Borasio)

86

Drenkel's Photographs

*T*hroughout most of the 1890s, D. R. Drenkel snapped photographs of Aspen's people, buildings, mines, and scenery. Shown here is one of Drenkel's bread-and-butter baby portraits. This infant wears a long-sleeved christening gown. The gown features eyelets around the bottom of the skirt and the bodice of the garment.

Drenkel solicited business with an ad (below) in the 1893 Aspen City Directory. (Denver Public Library, Western History Department) (Colorado Historical Society, Stephen Hart Library)

DRENKEL'S

FINEST · · · IN · · · ASPEN

Drenkel. Monarch St. Aspen, Colo.

SOUTH MONARCH STREET.

GALLERY ·209·

PHOTOGRAPHS

The written word

*I*magine life without television, movies, VCR's, and the Internet. Imagine the written word overshadowing most other forms of news and entertainment. Those were the days when Carbary's Corner Bookstore (right) did a brisk business. As indicated by the signs on the store building, shoppers could also purchase school books, ledgers, stationery, wallpaper, and toys. In later years Carbary's published a written and pictorial history of Aspen (below). (Both courtesy of Adeline Zupancis Kirsten)

ASPEN ILLUSTRATED.

.·. For Sale at Carbary's Corner Bookstore. .·.

Dry goods

Books, magazines, Indian rugs, pelts, photographs, light fixtures, and leather goods fill the interior of an unidentified Aspen dry goods store. (Denver Public Library, Western History Department)

Snow, Water Problems, and The New Camp of Creede

Monday, December 13, 1891. About 13 inches of new snow this morning. Worked all day. *Friday, December 17, 1891.* We went up to Camp today. Helped Robinsons move their machinery. They struck a great flow of water in their tunnel, and it did much damage. Washed away part of the works and blockaded the road, so teams can not get up or down from Ashcroft. *February 1, 1892.* At home all day. Lots of people going from here to the new camp, Creede, in the southern part of the state. *Monday, February 15, 1892.* Deposited $18.00 at First National Bank. I hired a team and Pete and I rode up home. Took some grub with us. (Armstrong's journals)

88

Saloons galore

*I*n 1891 Colorado law required saloons to close on Sunday. Aspen saloon owners ignored such foolishness. By 1892 the Aspen City Directory listed twenty seven saloons, including Madden's Saloon. Most drinking establishments used tokens (inset) as advertisements and to make change — that way customers would have to come back to "spend" the token. Token values usually ranged between 5 cents and 25 cents. (Aspen Historical Society) (Inset: Courtesy of Ed Borasio)

89

90

Unidentified Aspen homes

Charles Armstrong probably snapped both of these photographs. A woman stands in front of the modest home with a dormer window in the roof. Several adults and children look at the camera from in front of the more substantial home — possibly a ranch house. In 1891, Aspen builders constructed 320 new homes exceeding $1,000,000 in total value. (Armstrong's journals)

In Leadville, An Engine Off the Track, and Fine Swimming in Glenwood

Sunday, February 28, 1892. In Leadville with Sam Selden. Left Aspen 11 oclock last night by De&R.G.R.R. Got here about 6 oclock. Took breakfast at the Saddle Rock Restaurant. Looked over the town and surroundings till 5 P.M. We took the Midland train for home. Got to the wreck about 7 oclock.

Monday, February, 29, 1892. We were delayed till 8 oclock this morning at Sellers Station on the Frying Pan by an engine that was off the track.

Sunday, October 2, 1892. Bush and I went to Glenwood Springs today. Came back about midnight. Had a fine time swimming in the big pool. Saw John Watkins.

Saturday, October 15, 1892. Daubed the cabin today.

(Armstrong's journals)

Mr. and Mrs. Al Lamb

Prominent Aspen businessman Al Lamb and his wife sit on their front lawn with a litter of six retriever puppies. (Denver Public Library, Western History Department)

Luxurious living

*T*he Lamb family lived luxuriously. Three ornately decorated rooms in the Lamb house contain patterned wallpaper, ropes and tassels hanging from the entryways, a chandelier, wall paintings, book cases, velvet parlor chairs, straight-backed chairs, coffee tables, statues, a piano, and sculptures. Elaborate rugs cover the floors.

During winter, the Vulcan Fuel Company (above) supplied coal to help keep homes like the Lambs' cozy and warm. (Courtesy of P. David Smith) (Denver Public Library, Western History Department)

92

E. K. BUTTOLPH,

AGENT OF

THE VULCAN FUEL COMPANY.

ASPEN, COLO., July 31, 1893.

Al Lamb — Druggist

The Lambs lived well because of their successful drugstore. A master at marketing his business, Lamb played on his family name for over forty years. (Courtesy of Bill Ellicott) (Courtesy of Gary Bracken) (Courtesy of Adeline Zupancis Kirsten)

URE (your) Druggist is in business to render the special services that are required by each individual household in his community. The most vital of these special services is the sick call. Day or night—at any hour—Ure Druggist is at your service. Like your family physician he is a part of your home. Accuracy and Purity are Twins. :: ::

Albert Smith Lamb
PRESCRIPTION DRUGGIST

93

94

The evolution of a drugstore

*T*aken decades apart from similar
viewpoints, two photographs reveal
the evolution of Lamb's Drugstore.
(Courtesy of Adeline Zupancis Kirsten)
(Denver Public Library, Western History
Department)

Buyer beware

During the 1890s, Lamb had plenty of competition, including Knott's Pharmacy. Before the Food and Drug Act, pharmacies bottled (above) their own concoctions. Outrageous healing claims invariably accompanied the suspicious liquid remedies. A high alcoholic content made many of the claims come true, if only for a while. (Courtesy of Bill Ellicott) (Aspen City Directory, 1893)

GET YOUR PRESCRIPTIONS FILLED

AT

KNOTT'S PHARMACY

And Save 25 per cent.

BY PAYING CASH.

Purity of Drugs and Accuracy in Dispensing Guaranteed.

Knott's Red Spruce Gum and Wild Cherry Cough Syrup. A pure, wholesome syrup, free from injurious drugs, and which we guarantee to relieve any cough. Price 50 cents per bottle.

Knott's Lotus Balm for the Hands. When rubbed on the hands after washing it dries into the skin, leaving a smooth, silky feeling, healing all cracks, cuts, etc., and is quite free from stickiness. Price 25 cts. per bottle.

Knott's Little Giant Pills. The most pleasant cathartic or liver stimulant ever prepared. We guarantee these perfectly harmless to the most delicate constitution. Price 25 cents per bottle.

Knott's Beef, Iron and Wine Tonic is the most perfect preparation of this valuable tonic known. Price $1.00 per bottle.

Knott's Pharmacy, Cor. Galena and Cooper.

95

A Daisy of a Cabin, Insanity, and Cleveland Wins

Friday, October 21, 1892. Moved into our new cabin today. She is a daisy. Put up the stove & c. Ate supper in the new cabin.
Thursday, October 27, 1892. Went to Aspen today. I was on a jury to try a man by the name of Lee [?] for insanity. Found him insane. Pete came home with the horses and a 1/4 of beef. I went to lodge this evening.
Thursday, November 10, 1892. In town all day. Got some supplies at Clark & Denmans. Pete drove the outfit home this evening. Cleveland and the democrats swept the country by an over whelming majority. (Armstrong's journals)

96

For toothaches

In Charles Armstrong's 1905 - 1906 journal, he kept a cure for toothaches (above). The vagaries and pitfalls of nineteenth-century medicinal practices makes one thankful for the more modern, albeit not always perfect, scientific approach. (Armstrong's journals)

Mourning A Companion

Tuesday, December 20, 1892. Cold and snowing. Old Bear [Armstrong's dog] seems to be sick. Won't eat and dumps around the house. Chas. Hubbard took dinner with me. He came from Italian Mt.
Wednesday, December 21, 1892. Poor, faithful, Old Bear lay on the floor dead this morning. He must have got a dose of poison night before last. I have been mourning over him all day. I raised him from a puppy. He was born in 1883. And there has hardly been a day that we have not been together in all that time.
Thursday, December 22, 1892. I feel very lonesome and sad about Old Bear dying. He has been such a faithful old comrade all these years.
Friday, December 23, 1892. Washing clothes today. Fine sunny day. Cut a lock of hair off Old Bear's tail to remember him. I had no idea that I loved that old dog so. (Armstrong's journals)

For the seriously ill

*F*or those not cured by pharmaceutical concoctions, a modern three-story hospital awaited them. In the early 1890s, Aspen's Citizens Hospital (both views) had a tower with a hipped roof at its entrance, gables, dormer windows, chimneys, and a balcony on each of two wings. Over a dozen physicians made use of this state-of-the-art facility.

Men maimed by mining accidents and suffering from "black lung disease" filled many of the beds. For them the next stop was often the Evergreen or Red Butte Cemetery. Six of every 1,000 Colorado miners died from work-related accidents during the Victorian era. Unsanitary living conditions also spawned epidemics of typhoid, diphtheria, smallpox, and scarlet fever. (Courtesy of Adeline Zupancis Kirsten) (Courtesy of Beck family collection)

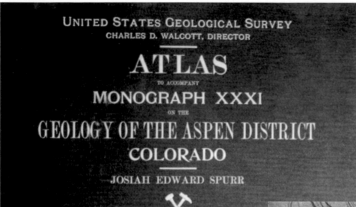

Aspen mines

By early 1893, Pitkin Country boasted over 227 active mines and 2,500 professional miners. A United States Geological Survey map of the Aspen Mining District (above) shows most of the biggest producing mines close to downtown Aspen.

During this heady time, Aspen advocates could hardly contain themselves: "This county [Pitkin] produced last year one-sixth of the silver of the United States, and its history has but commenced. No place in the world shows such a sure chance for the investment of capital in mines" (Canfield, 1893). (Both courtesy of Leo Stambaugh)

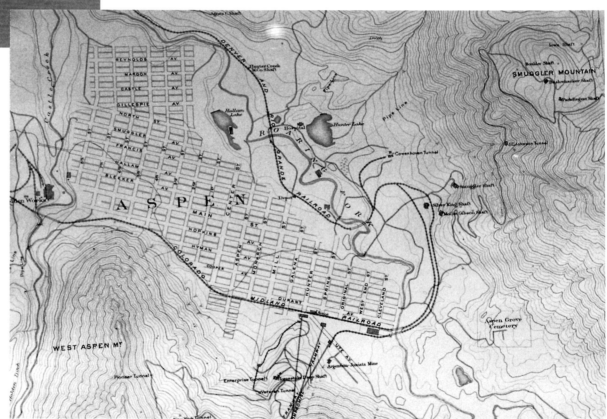

Bushwacker Mine

During his career in Aspen, Frank Bulkley (left) managed several mines, including Jerome Wheeler's Bushwacker Mine (below). Located on twenty acres of patented ground, the "Bushwacker was incorporated under the laws of the state of Colorado in April, 1890, with a capital stock divided into 2,000,000 shares of the par value of $1" (Canfield, 1893). Timber piled outside the shaft house probably provided fuel for a steam-operated boiler inside. (Lake Country Public Library)

99

100

First electric hoist

"**T**here is no old fogy mining going on here. It was the first camp that adopted the use of electricity in mining [Telluride historians would dispute this claim]. The first electric hoist ever made was for an Aspen mine" (Canfield, 1893). (Crane, 1913)

More Promises, Fine Winter, Poor Sleighing, and Another Deadly Snowslide

Sunday, January 1, 1893. No more treating nor drinking in Aspen. No more smoking, but business and rational pleasure.
Wednesday, January 25, 1893. Warm and springlike this morning. We are having the finest winter I ever saw in this country.
Thursday, January 26, 1893. Rode to Aspen with Morris. Sleighing is poor. All the hillsides are bare. Stopped at the Clarendon for Supper Bed & Breakfast. Went to Lodge this evening.
Friday, February 3, 1893. Clear today. Got the mail. There were two men killed near Aspen Wednesday by a snow slide. This seems to have been a general storm all over the western country. We did not work today, but sat around the house and read papers. (Amrstrong's journals)

Five miles of tunnels

Workers in the Park-Regent Mine operate a rare compressed-air drill. "The principal development of the property [Park-Regent] consists of two vertical shafts, each about 500 feet in depth. From these shafts, inclines and levels have been driven in the veins. The total underground development of the property exceeds five miles in length . . . . At the present time three hoisting engines of 75 combined horse-power and boilers aggregating 150 horse-power are in use" (Canfield, 1893). (Lake County Public Library)

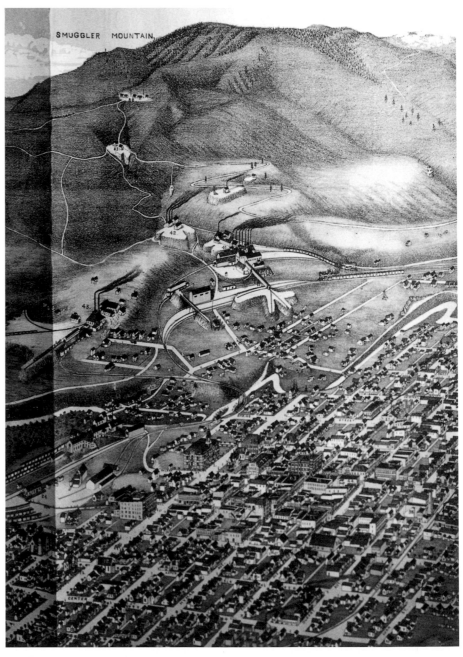

"Sights that compare with the seven wonders of the world"

*T*ucked against the base of Smuggler Mountain (left edge of image darkened by old fold) on the eastern edge of town, the mighty Smuggler (42), Mollie Gibson (43), and Cowenhoven Tunnel (44) loom like giant sentinels over the city. "The Commercial Club invites you to visit any or all of them . . . . [descend] the Smuggler shaft 1,200 feet, see the mammoth plants pumping 2,000 gallons of water a minute . . . these are sights that compare with the seven wonders of the world" (Aspen Commercial Club booklet: undated). (Courtesy of Ben Kirsten)

102

Richer than King Solomon's mines

"*T*here have been articles innumerable written about this treasure house of almost inexhaustible riches; but there never has nor will there ever be one which can possibly portray accurately or even give a faint idea of the real wonder and vastness of this silver [The Mollie Gibson Mine] deposit, the like unto which King Solomon nor the much written-about Aztecs never feasted their eyes upon" (Canfield, 1893). (Aspen Commercial Club booklet: undated)

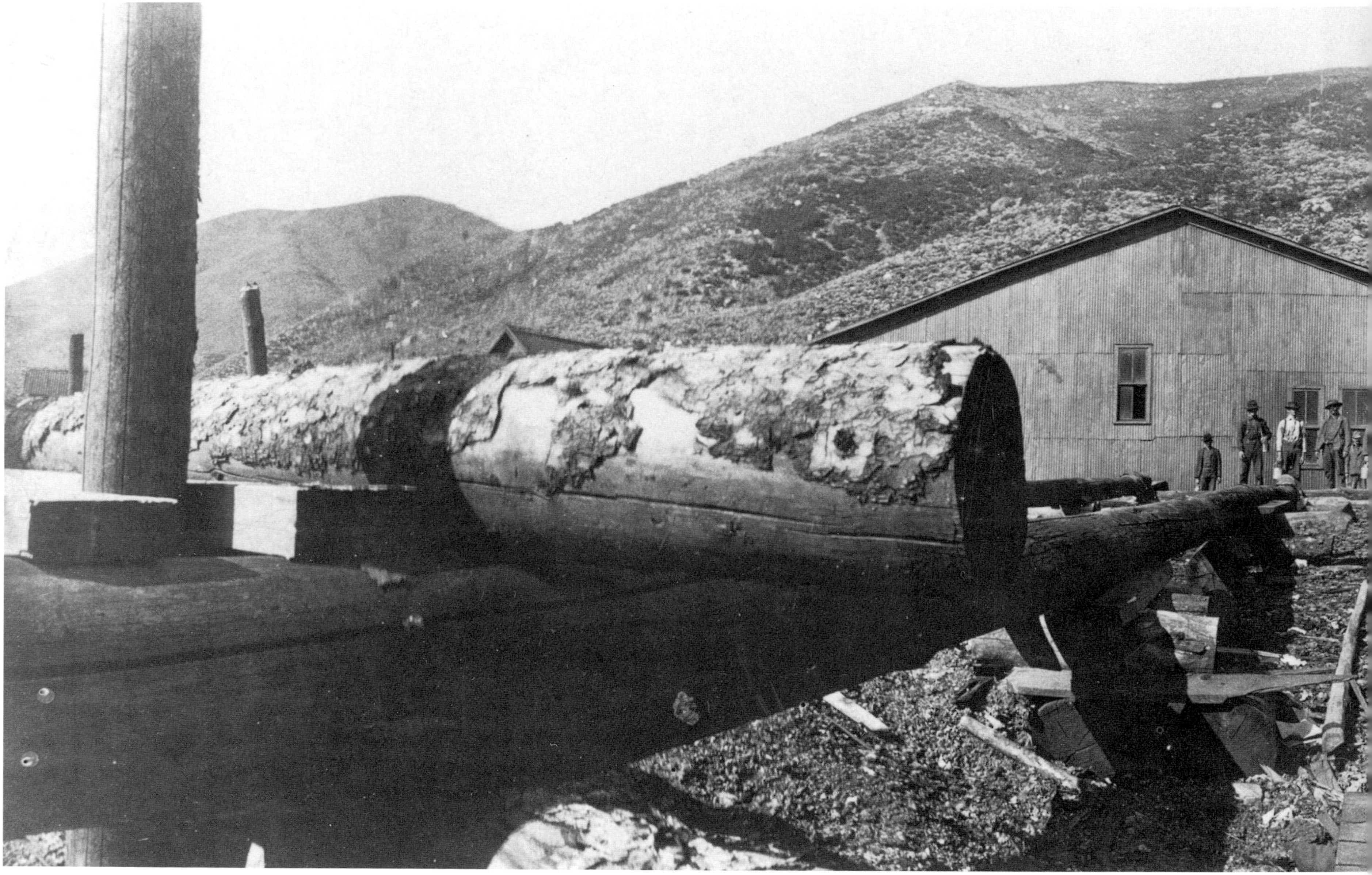

The mighty Smuggler

*O*ne of Aspen's richest and longest-operating mines, the Smuggler (left) "was incorporated under the laws of West Virginia, with a capital stock of $100,000, divided into shares of the par value of $10 per share. The officers and directors are Charles J. Hughes, Jr., president; D. M. Hyman, vice president, and Charles A. Hallam, general manager. The Smuggler mine was first discovered in 1879, and its location is in Aspen, adjoining the Mollie Gibson mines . . . . For the year 1892 the mine produced 29,967 tons of ore, the receipts from which amounted to $350,696.88" (Canfield, 1893). (Museum of Western Colorado)

107

108

Smuggler hoist room

Adorned with an eye-catching array of theatrical posters, the Smuggler hoist room (above) housed powerful equipment that lowered hundreds of miners into the bowels of the earth. Deep in the Smuggler, four well-dressed men (inset) appear to be inspecting a stope in the "17th, 18th, and 19th stories [levels]" (Canfield, 1893). (Aspen Historical Society) (Lake County Public Library)

World's largest nuggets

*I*n 1893 miners in the Mollie Gibson Mine discovered a 1,840 pound silver nugget, the largest in the world. A year later, as though not to be outdone by their close rival, miners on Level 5 of the Smuggler Mine uncovered a 2,350 pound nugget of 93% pure silver. Excited miners had to break it into three pieces to get it out. The monster nugget netted nearly $21,000 for the owners of the Smuggler Mine. Above, a miner, his son, and dog pose on a horse-drawn wagon with the three hunks of the newly crowned "world's largest nugget." (Denver Public Library, Western History Department)

110

Aspen at its frenetic best

A few years before the silver crash, this stereoview captures the south side of Aspen at its frenetic best — a jack train readies to depart, people dressed in traveling clothes hustle by, railroad cars line the tracks, and new construction on the Aspen Sampling Company towers over the chaos. (Author's collection)

5570. Loading the great Burro Train, Aspen, Col., U. S. A.

Copyright 1890, by B. W. Kilburn.

The Little Annie Mine, Moving to Aspen, Still Prospecting, and Still Drinking

Monday, September 18, 1893. Pete went to work on the Little Annie Mine [for] $2.50 a day & board.

Tuesday, November 21, 1893. We moved to Aspen today. Bob Long hauled us down. Charged $2.50. Pete paid him. We are in John Coll's house.

Monday, November 27, 1893. Out prospecting all day. Did not see any gold and don't believe there is any.

Saturday, December 23, 1893. Splendid weather we are having. I have been fooling away the past 3 days with Don Kennedy. He came to town from Tourtelotte Park Tuesday and has been drunk every since. He stopped with me 3 nights, but I hope I have got rid of him till he sobers up.

Wednesday, February 21, 1894. There is nothing new in the camp. Silver keeps going down. It is 63 1/4 c for oz now. I am very much afraid that it will go so low that the mines will shut down. There is gold excitement below Aspen Junction and quite a number went down night before last to see what it amounted to. (Armstrong's journals)

Smelters

Aspen depended on its mills and samplers to process the ore from the mines. This classic image shows a line of freight wagons and a train beside the Aspen Sampling Works. "The capacity of the works is 250 tons daily, of ten hours, giving steady employment to thirty-five men, and is perfectly equipped with all modern mechanical facilities for the most careful and economical operation" (Canfield, 1893). The 1893 Aspen City Directory lists five ore-processing plants, although these primitive ore separation facilities should not be confused with smelters like those in Leadville and Denver that refined ore into silver. (Colorado Historical Society, Stephen Hart Library)

Lixiviation

Men in the mining industry constantly sought better and cheaper methods for extracting precious metal from ore. "The new Holden Smelting and Milling Company's plant [below] for treating ore by the Russell process of lixiviation is a new industry. The building covers 12,000 square feet of ground and has a capacity of 125 tons per day" (Canfield, 1893). A bird's eye view drawn in 1893 shows the plant at its peak (right). "The works treated one hundred tons a day,

113

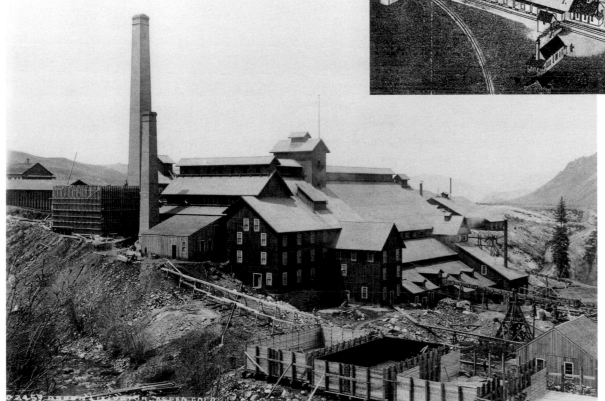

including some ore shipped across the mountains from Leadville, a circumstance that gave Aspenites enormous psychic satisfaction after so many years a poor relation" (Rohrbough, 1986). The Holden 'Lixiviation' Works only operated from 1891 to 1893.

One can still visit the site, now a historic mining and ranching interpretive center on the west edge of Aspen. Only the building immediately to the right of the number "7" (above) remains. (Courtesy of Ben Kirsten) (Colorado Historical Society, Stephen Hart Library)

Cinder and smoke

Deadly pollution spewed by mines, mills, and samplers plagued Aspen's environment for years. This view of Aspen is taken from the north. A line of train cars are in the foreground. Cinder and smoke from the Aspen Sampler, the Sampler, and the Argentum-Juniata at the base of Aspen Mountain blanket the city. (University of Wyoming, American Heritage Center)

114

Taking stock

"*A*t the mines, the men are given the choice of taking their pay in cash or in corporation stock. Almost without exception they take their wages in stock, reserving only enough ready cash to keep them in tobacco and postage-stamps. The company pays their board. Under this arrangement the miners feel that they have an actual interest in the result of their labor" (*Harper's Weekly,* January 19, 1889). Local Aspen historian, Larry Fredrick, takes exception to this account. He notes that in the large Aspen mines only a few powerful persons tightly controlled the stock. Fredrick also points out that after the silver crash, B. Clark Wheeler (see next page) proved to be an exception, paying his Little Annie workers half their wages in stock, and half in cash. Smaller mines often made their stock available to the general public, although most miners could not afford a single share.

"This [right: J. F. MacMillan] business firm was the first of the kind to start in Aspen, in the year 1884 . . . . In earlier transactions of their business they confined it exclusively to silver mining stocks, but a large and constantly increasing clientage [certainly not miners] in the east, and in Canada as well, called for gold mining stock investments" (Canfield, 1893). MacMillan handled over thirty local mines stocks. Note the "Free Coinage" banner hanging from a giant set of elk antlers. (Courtesy of Adeline Zupancis Kirsten) (Inset: Lake County Public Library)

J. F. MACMILLAN,

(Member Colorado Mining Stock Exchange,)

Mines, ————— ⚜

Mining Stocks,

Bonds and Warrants.

CORRESPONDENCE SOLICITED.

403 HYMAN AVE.,

ASPEN, COLO.

Reference:
First National Bank
of Aspen.

P. O. BOX 153.

115

HISTORIC ASPEN IN RARE PHOTOGRAPHS

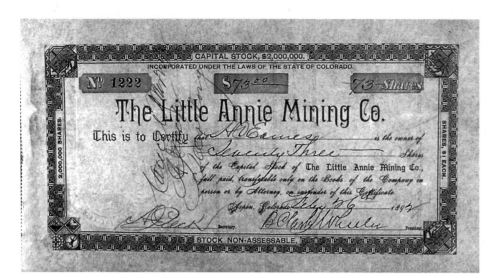

The Little Annie Mining Company

*E*ver the entrepreneur, B. Clark Wheeler bought the Little Annie and issued stock to finance its development. Wheeler personally signed the stock certificates (left). "Wheeler developed a scheme under which miners worked for the customary $3.00 a day, $1.50 paid in cash, the remainder in eight shares of stock valued at twenty-five cents each. That he succeeded is selling his stock to workers above and below ground was a tribute to his resourcefulness and the spell cast by the rumors of great wealth" (Rohrbough, 1986). (Courtesy of Ralph Kemper)

116

"Sold the Ranch to B. Clark Wheeler for $6,500"

*O*n Saturday, February 13, 1892, Armstrong wrote (right) that he *sold the Ranch to B. Clark Wheeler for $6,500.* The exact location and size of the "ranch" is unknown. It may have been close to, or even part of, Clark's Little Annie Mining properties. Although both Armstrong and Wheeler worried about falling silver prices, neither could have imagined that the demise of mining in Aspen would come so soon. By the end of 1893 most mines in the vicinity would be closed, the bottom would fall out of real estate prices, and silver-mine stocks would be worthless. (Armstrong's journals)

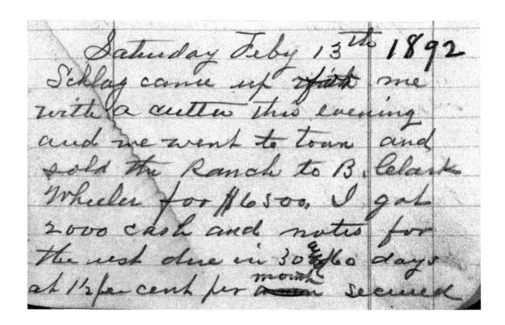

Copyright 1893, by B. W. Kilburn.

8166. Aspen's Silver Queen, Colorado Mining Building, Columbian Exposition.

Soon silver would not be queen

*A*s the city and mining center of Aspen came into its own during the early 1890s, they had one overriding reason for optimism: the rich silver deposits in the earth below them seemed inexhaustible. Yet some powerful Easterners kept clamoring for the repeal of the Sherman Silver Purchase Act, which had buoyed silver prices for years.

In 1892 Aspen decided that the world needed a spectacular reminder — in the form of a "Silver Queen" — that silver's worth and appeal equaled gold's. The city, charging citizens 50 cents to see her to help foot the bill (the full amount was never paid), built the Silver Queen (above) and shipped it to the 1893 Chicago's World Fair. "The principal idea of the statue, the parity of silver and gold, was symbolized by two winged gods who were drawing the chariot. Each carried a cornucopia; one poured forth gold; the other, silver. The Silver Queen's head and the eagle were carved from solid silver nuggets. The height of the exhibit was eighteen feet, and the base measured ten feet by twelve. The cost of the statue was $10,000, but its silver message failed" (Bancroft, 1954). (Courtesy of Joann Leech)

Wonders of the 1893 Chicago World's Fair

[Armstrong is now at the 1893 Chicago World's Fair, having stopped there on his way back from visiting his family in Arkport, New York. Curiously, he never mentions seeing the Silver Queen statue, Aspen' s contribution to the fair — perhaps because there were so many wonders to see.]

Tuesday, June 27, 1893. Out to the World's Fair this evening. Grand Electric display. I got back home at 10 P.M. The fair is immense, the trouble is there is so much that a person is confused.

Sunday, July 2, 1893. Went to the fair. Was in the art gallery most of the day. Saw the Old Dewit Clinton Locomotive and coaches used on the Hudson & Skenectada [?] R.R. in 1831. Fir mast at the door of the Washington Building is 215 ft high and only 3 1/2 ft in diameter.

Monday, July 3, 1893. Walked through the Illinois Building, the Government Bldg and Krups [?] exhibit and the Leather Exhibit. Saw leather belt 12 ft wide, [and] another [one] two miles long. Saw Redwood plank in Forestry building 16 ft & 5 in wide & 5 inches thick. Ate lunch in the Big Tree Restaurant. They use the Big Tree for a counter. It is 4ft square & 111 ft. long, and weighs 92,000 lbs & is 442 years old. Went to Buffalo Bill's show this evening.

Tuesday, July 4, 1893. An immense crowd on the fair ground today. The celebration did not amount to much. Big fireworks in the evening. I got home 12:45. Saw Charley Fields from Aspen and was around with him. In the evening, saw Persian Dancing girls on the Midway Plaisance & c.

Thursday, July 6, 1893. Was at the Fair today. Saw silver filigree model of the Horticultural Hall, made in Monterey Mexico, using 11lbs of silver. [It is] 11 ft 2 inches long [and] 3ft 2 1/2 inches wide. Represents the labor of 12 men, 13 months at 18 hours a day. Took in the Ferris wheel [for] 50c. Also the Streets of Cairo [for] 15c. Also the English soldier tournament [for] 50c. All good.

Friday, July 7, 1893. The Caravels came in this afternoon and they received quite an ovation. The parade was good. U.S. soldiers, English soldiers & sailors, Indians, South Sea Islanders, Eskimos, Dahomans, Bedouins, & c, & c. I was up on the promenade on Manufacturers Building. [It is] 140 ft high and 1/2 mile around. Fine view, cost 25c. Saw a Tarpon from Florida — 7 ft 2 in long and weighted 205lbs. Saw the Tiffany diamond worth $100,000. Also [saw] Gorman's silver statue of Columbus — valued at $50,000. Was in the Libby glass works this evening [for] 10c.

Saturday, July 8, 1893. Went to fair this afternoon Took in the Bedouin encampment. Also Old Vienna. Saw the fireworks this evening. They were first class. Stopped afterwards to hear the Cincinnati Band play. They are fine. Monday, July 10, 1893. At the fair. Saw a chunk of huge native copper, weighted 8,500lbs. Another weighted 6,200lbs from Central Mine Mich. Saw the Kimberly South Africa diamond exhibit, diamonding washing, and rough diamonds, also cutting the stones.

Tuesday, July 11, 1893. Was downtown. Had a long talk with Arthur Woodcock. Was in Libby Prison this afternoon, 50c admission. Lots of relics of the War. The bed that Lincoln died on — the sheet soaked with his blood, [and] trees full of bullets & shells. Two miniballs that met in mid air and were flattened out and welded together, & c & c. Well worth the money.

Wednesday, July 12, 1893. In Blarney Castle refreshment room getting away with a bottle of beer and a cheese sandwich = 25c. Admission 25c. Did not kiss the Blarney stone. It is only a piece about 6 by 8 in. Costs 10c to kiss it. It looks as though a million people had slobbered over it. (Armstrong's journals)

Not even Aspen's own, Governor Davis Waite, could save silver

*I*n July 1893 the United States repealed the Sherman Silver Purchase Act. Silver prices plummeted overnight. Stunned Aspenites could not believe it. What took almost 15 years of hard labor and massive capital to build, collapsed almost overnight. Within days of the sudden fall in the price of silver, most silver mines in the Aspen Mining District — and across the state — shut down. The closures sent devastating economic ripples throughout every Colorado community.

    Even one of Aspen's most prominent citizens, Davis Waite, the first Colorado Governor to sit in the new State Capitol building (1893 - 1895), could do nothing to prevent the repeal. Waite, like most Western governors, carried little political weight back east. The silver boom was over. Aspen's doom had been sealed. (Lake County Public Library)

Bread-lines and bankruptcy

*B*y the end of 1893, bread-lines formed in Denver and eighty percent of Aspen's mines and businesses faced bankruptcy. Many Aspenites headed for the Cripple Creek gold fields. Although the Crystal City's population still hovered around 5,000, downtown Aspen no longer bustled. An unwelcome quiet enveloped the Aspen Block on the corner of Galena Street and Hyman Avenue in the heart of the business district (above). (Denver Public Library, Western History Department)

Empty streetcars

Since the 1880s, Aspen's public streetcars conveniently and safely ferried passengers from one end of town to the other. Although they were never well used and operated only in the summer, they served as a source of community pride. In the top view a lone streetcar makes its way down the rails on a nearly deserted Mill Street. Below, two streetcars, each drawn by one horse, stand empty — a common sight after 1893. In 1899 the city tore out the tracks. (Courtesy of Adeline Zupancis Kirsten) (Denver Public Library, Western History Department)

120

Famous Ashcroft Mining Camp near Aspen, Colo.

Ashcroft: Population 50

High above Aspen, Ashcroft looked like a ghost town. The 1896 Colorado State Business Directory generously listed a population of 50, two businesses, and a tri-weekly stage to Aspen (passed close to Armstrong's cabin). Even the man with the Midas touch, H. A. W. Tabor, lost his considerable investments in the Tam O'Shanter and Montezuma Mines near Ashcroft. (Courtesy of Ralph Kemper)

121

122

Supposed gold camp

During summer, miners packed into high-country "camps" (inset). On July 18, 1895, Charles Armstrong drew this map (left) of a *supposed gold camp* on upper Difficult Creek. Armstrong made numerous trips to this camp, and others, from his cabin on Castle Creek below Ashcroft. He rode through Ashcroft, often stopping for liquid refreshments, then continued on the Taylor Pass wagon road until he reached the cutoff to the headwaters of Difficult Creek.

In the fall of 1999, the author and two friends, Bill Ellicott and Scott Strain, searched for Armstrong's *supposed gold camp*. (Courtesy of Joann Leech) (Armstrong's journals)

It laid out exactly like Armstrong's 1895 map

After several hours and numerous wrong turns, we negotiated a rough 4-wheel drive track just above timberline at the head of Difficult Creek. We examined a copy of Armstrong's map as we surveyed the small, picturesque valley. Incredibly, the location of the structural remnants appeared to lay out exactly like Armstrong's century-old map. There was, however, one oddity that raised some doubt. Armstrong had drawn a small "MILL" (center, toward the bottom of the map) with a peaked roof and a column of smoke drifting from its chimney duct. No mill we had ever seen had a peaked roof. Mills have step-like roofs, reflecting the refining operations inside.

We hiked down into the valley. Eagerly, we peered inside the peaked "MILL" building (above). Hazy light passed through gaps in the roof, illuminating a five-stamp mill operation (left). (Author's photos)

Less ore and fewer trains

*I*n 1894, with the overall mining production in Aspen less than half that of 1892, the Denver and Rio Grande Railroad and the Colorado Midland Railway cut back their schedules. Above, three men, two boys, and a large dog gather around and on a hand cart used for track inspection and maintenance. A water tower with a bell-shaped tin roof stands alongside the track at Woody Creek about sixteen miles north of Aspen. (Denver Public Library, Western History Department)

Hot Springs excursions

Riding the rails through the gorgeous Roaring Fork Valley to the salubrious hot springs water in Glenwood Springs remained popular with Aspenites, but it could not sustain a railroad. (Both from author's collection)

5624. Fun for the boys, Glenwood Springs, Col., U. S. A.

Copyright 1890, by B. W. Kilburn.

125

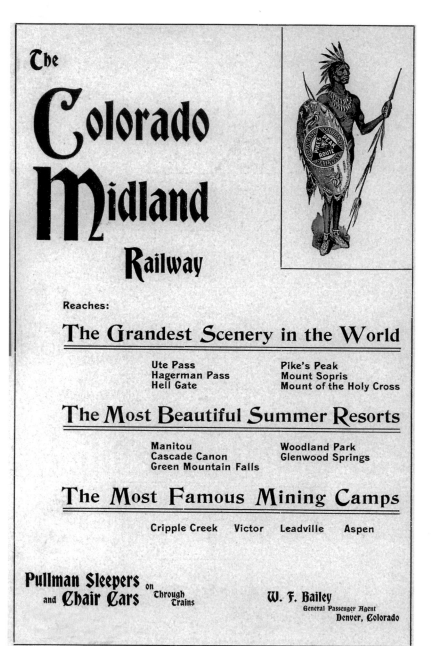

126

The Colorado Midland Railway hangs on

*T*he Colorado Midland Railway never realized large profits. After the silver crash it hung on, although barely, until October 1921, when its standard-gauge rails were torn up and the company dissolved. A Midland ad (left) and first-class ticket (below) are shown here. The railway's logo, an Indian holding a shield, became famous throughout Colorado and the West. (Courtesy of P. David Smith) (Courtesy of Adeline Zupancis Kirsten)

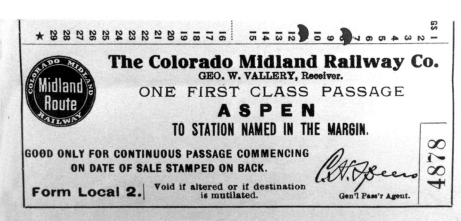

Warriors no more

*T*his version of the Colorado Midland "Indian logo" might have looked good on railroad literature, but it did not correspond to reality. (Colorado Historical Society, Stephen Hart Library)

128

Poverty and squalor

*B*y the time the Colorado Midland track reached Aspen in 1887, most Ute Indians lived on reservations (in southern Colorado and southern Utah) in poverty and squalor. Above, in about 1880, a group of Utes at the Los Pinos agency watch cattle being butchered. In the foreground a Ute woman is on her hands and knees near a pile of intestines. (Colorado Historical Society, Stephen Hart Library)

"The cyclone of civilization"

*T*he expressions on the faces of these two Ute women (left) reflect the harshness of the land and the hopelessness of their condition. From the inset, Chief Ouray stares forlornly.

In 1893 Chief Simon Pokagon, a Potawatomi Chief, was invited to speak at the "Columbian Fair" in Chicago. He refused. Instead, he wrote these words: "In behalf of my people, the American Indians, I hereby declare to you, the pale-faced race that has usurped our lands and homes, that we have no spirit to celebrate with you the great Columbia Fair now being held in the Chicago city, the wonder of the world . . . [No] sooner had the news reached the Old World that a new continent had been found, peopled with another race of men, then locust-like, they swarmed on all our coasts. The cyclone of civilization spread westward; the forests of untold centuries were swept away; streams dried up; lakes fell back from their ancient bounds; and all our fathers once loved to gaze upon was destroyed, defaced, or marred, except the sun, moon, and starry skies above, which the Great Spirit in his wisdom hung beyond their reach" (Pokagon, 1893). (Crane, 1913)

129

Hell Gate

One wonders why the Colorado Midland did not choose a scenic logo. Hell Gate on the west slope of Hagerman Pass (above) is 3,000 feet above the Frying Pan River at an altitude of 10,540 feet. For thirty-five years this magnificent stretch left Midland passengers awed and breathless. (Crane, 1913)

Spending Money Foolishly, The *Maine* Explodes, and Attitudes toward Alaska

Thursday, September 30, 1897. I got $2.55 worth of groceries and came up with the stage. I spent $4.10 last night foolishly, and today I am kicking myself for it.

Wednesday, October 20, 1897. I caught one fish, after fishing most of the day. My back troubles me yet. I sent to Aspen after a plaster by Mr. Saunders this morning [for] 25cts. Fine sunny day.

Tuesday, February 15, 1898. U. S. Battleship Maine blowed up at 9:45 this evening in Havana harbor, Cuba.

Tuesday, April 26, 1898. War [Spanish-American] is declared, so the mail man says.

Monday, August 1, 1898. Dan Bruce and Mr. Bollum came back from Alaska Saturday. We had a long talk with them today. They gave it a hard name and say they don't want any more of it.

(Armstrong's journals)

A high-country sculpture

Another possibility for the Colorado Midland logo, the Hagerman trestle ranked as one of the most spectacular feats in American railroading. Not only was the wooden trestle a monumental engineering feat, its graceful lines and powerful bearing made it a high-country sculpture. (Colorado Historical Society, Stephen Hart Library)

131

Summer and winter

*I*vanhoe, a Colorado Midland station by Ivanhoe Lake, appears in summer and winter. In the summer view notice the "Western Union Telegraph & Cable Office" sign, along with "Colo. Springs 56.8 Miles," and "Aspen 59.4." Winter reeked havoc upon the Colorado Midland Railway. Snowslides frequently covered the tracks. Deep snows left trains buried for days. Come spring, melting snow washed out bridges and long sections of grade.

Imagine working at remote Ivanhoe Station during long Colorado winters. (Both from Denver Public Library, Western History Department)

133

Keeping the tracks open

K eeping the tracks open demanded extraordinary vigilance and effort on the part of the Denver and Rio Grande Railroad, too (above). It was also expensive. Rotary snowplows like this one (shown in a faded photograph) often malfunctioned, causing delays for hours and sometimes days. (Author's collection)

Winter wasn't all bad

*F*or some free-spirited Aspenites, winter wasn't all bad. Of course, skiing served mainly a utilitarian purpose: getting from one place to another. Yet some miners seemed to enjoy it more than others, racing one another (above) down from the mines after their long shifts. Some locals even formed ski clubs, staging races between neighboring camps. (Aspen Historical Society)

The end of the nineteenth century

From 1879 to 1893 Aspen had had an incredible run. So had the United States. By the end of the nineteenth century, however, the world had changed dramatically. The industrial revolution, new technology, improved communication, and faster transportation resulted in increased contact among countries and continents. Add chauvinism and imperialism to the mix and one has a deadly brew laced with the certainty of conflict.

By the turn of the century, Charles Armstrong had spent twenty years in the Aspen vicinity. His 1899 mosaic of impressions (right) combines several poignant visual representations of that era: tents, trees, battleships, human faces, a rabbit, an oculus, bees, mosquitos, cannons, and bursting shells. (Armstrong's journals)

135

CHAPTER THREE
The Crystal City Languishes
(1900s-1910s)

Although Aspen did not have much to cheer about, its citizens celebrated the beginning of the twentieth century with enthusiasm. Guns roared, bells rang, and thundering fireworks streaked across the mountain sky. Giddy celebrants filled the streets to drink and dance their way into the new century. Not everyone, however, cared to join the rowdy crowds. Charles Armstrong, now fifty-three years old, does not even mention the advent of the new century in his journals.

In 1900 the boom years seemed more distant than seven years ago to the remaining 3,300 Aspen citizens. Since the silver crash of 1893, the city had taken an economic beating. By the early 1900s almost half of the businesses had closed. The public trolley tracks were torn out. Fewer trains chugged in and out of town. In 1901 everyone understood the implications when Jerome B. Wheeler, Aspen's stalwart community leader and financial savior since the early 1880s, declared bankruptcy. The few mines that remained open struggled to keep afloat financially. In 1905 miners' wages at the Park Regent and Bushwacker Mines were reduced to $2.50 per day. In 1906 the Colorado Midland Railway went bankrupt, although it continued to operate at a loss. By 1908 only the Smuggler Mine, which had taken over several other patented claims, remained open.

Not only the economy was bad. Long ago Aspen had also sacrificed its appealing mountain environment to the silver gods. The frenetic boom years left an ugly and toxic legacy. Rather than magnificent stands of trees, a sea of stumps stuck out from the surrounding foothills. Among the stumps, massive mounds of bright-colored earth had been churned up and spit out helter-skelter — giving the appearance of a giant gopher colony. A few unsightly slag piles lay abandoned on the south end of the valley. People feared that toxic ooze from the samplers, smelters, and

concentrators would seep into the earth and major waterways. Each year the number of abandoned buildings and homes, with weathered boards nailed over broken windows, increased. The once proud Wheeler Opera House stood vacant, gutted by two suspicious fires in 1912. Taken altogether, this did not fit one's image of an idyllic mountain town.

By 1910 residents of the Roaring Fork Valley started to turn a material eye toward its farming and ranching legacy. Within the boundaries of Pitkin County over 45,000 acres of producing farm and ranch land, although not in the same league with silver bonanzas, bode well for the future of a devastated local economy. Gradually, more acreage was planted, more cattle brought in, and more barbed wire strung. Many locals believed that ranching and farming in the fertile Roaring Fork Valley offered Aspen its best chance of economic stability.

Other people decided to bolster the local economy by attracting more "motoring tourists." It did not take a genius to see that America had quickly embraced a new traveling wonder: the automobile. Around 1904 the first "automobile waggons," as Charles's Armstrong labeled them, chugged noisily into Aspen. They frightened the horses and gouged dangerous ruts in the streets. Since these self-powered technological monstrosities were clearly unfit for mountain travel, many Aspenites never expected to see any more of them. They were wrong. Within a decade motorized "wagons" poured into Aspen, Colorado, and the West. Everyone wanted one of these newfangled mechanical contraptions, or so it seemed. They became so popular that the State of Colorado, and even a few private individuals, started to build mountain roads to accommodate them. By 1911 the newly created State Highway Department designated the Independence Pass road from Leadville to Aspen (which closely followed the trail of the original pioneers) as an official "State Highway." In 1912 the Forest Service allocated $2,000 to improve the highway, although the first vehicle would not pass over the summit until 1922. Aspen businesses printed postcards and folders proclaiming the region, in essence, the new haven for automobile enthusiasts.

Aspen also stepped up its efforts to lure tourists who liked to fish and hunt, especially in an inviting mountain environment (if far enough from the abandoned mills and mines). Tourist brochures and picture postcards featured full creels and successful big-game hunting camps. Local and state government supported efforts to "reclaim" sections of the polluted Roaring Fork River. In 1913, a shipment of elk meant to replenish the depleted elk population made local headlines when it arrived at the Aspen depot in a Denver and Rio Grande stock car.

Did these efforts to attract tourists succeed? More people and "Car Clubs" made excursions to Aspen from nearby towns like Leadville and Glenwood Springs. So too, more fishermen appeared on the streams and more hunters trekked into the surrounding mountains. But the overall influx of tourists remained small, especially during the long winter. Even during the summer months, tourists did not even come close to being the Crystal City's economic salvation.

In 1917, as many of Aspen's young men marched off to war in Europe, its economy continued to spiral downward. As if things were not bad enough, during the fall of 1918 the world-wide flu epidemic struck Aspen with a vengeance. In less than a month, one out of every forty residents died. No person who had flu-like symptoms was allowed to vote. Public meetings were banned. Schools closed.

Clearly, Aspen struggled just to survive during the first two decades of the twentieth century. By 1919 Aspen's population had dwindled to fewer than 1,500. Nevertheless, look closely at the faces of the people who appear in the following photographs. Their expressions, whether they are on a picnic or drumming up business for the local playhouse, tend to belie the hard times they faced. The pride Aspen took in its fire-hose team, baseball team, and high school athletes is apparent in the participants' postures. Moreover, people in general seemed to be enjoying life in Aspen — surely a tribute to human resiliency.

Interviews I conducted with first-generation descendants of Aspen families confirm this. They all recounted hearing about the hard economic times, the horrible human toll exacted by the flu epidemic, and the town's disheartening physical demise. Then they shared photographs of smiling relatives who, despite the difficulties they faced, relished living in Aspen's mountain environment. Never did I hear that anyone's relative wanted to leave Aspen. When they left, and most eventually did, it was only because they had to.

137

138

Locating Claims and A Crazy Preacher

Monday, January 1, 1900. Located 3 claims near the house for McMillen. Pete & I went up to the Caverhill Mine early this morning & I located another claim for Mc. And we dug about 1/2 [of a] location cut by 10 oclock and came home. Splendid day.

Friday, April 6, 1900. Fine this morning. And I took a stroll up above the Tenderfoot. Stormy the rest of the day. An Itinerant preacher, Elmer Jennison, strolled in this afternoon out of the storm and stopped with me. He's a good talker and preaches for the good of his fellowman. Crazy I guess. He has been all over the southern & western part of Colo. Has been down in the White River Country, and is bound for Gunnison "for the good of souls." He is man about 35 years of age. Not afraid of work. (Armstrong's journals)

Aspen struggles

With Smuggler and Aspen Mountains in the background, Aspen still appeared like the Crystal City of old. But it was not. After the turn of the century people continued to leave in droves. Most of the mines closed. Smoke no longer hung over the city. Businesses struggled to survive. (Courtesy of Ben Kirsten)

An unusual view of downtown

A "Hardware" sign can barely be seen on the building to the far left. It was the first masonry structure in Aspen. The large brick building behind the flag pole is the Independence Building (then called the Brown and Hoag Building), anchor of the Brown and Hoag Block. Tomkins Hardware's long narrow roof angles away from the viewer in the left foreground. The flat-roofed building in the center housed the Buckhorn Saloon. To the far right, the Brick Saloon's (now The Red Onion) odd-shaped roof leads one's eye to the fire-bell tower. Aspen Mountain looms above the city. (Courtesy of Ben Kirsten)

140

"Like the sunny stretches of Kansas"

*I*n 1889 a popular illustrated magazine predicted: "The agricultural area necessary to support the population that eventually will fill the country is close at hand. The Roaring Fork Valley [above] and the prolific valley of the Grand [present-day Colorado] need only proper cultivation to make them yield crops like the sunny stretches of Kansas. Farmers here will not have to send their products through the Hagerman Tunnel or over the Tennessee Pass, for their market will be in the mountains all about them" (*Harper's Weekly*, January 19, 1889).

Until 1893 this prophecy proved correct. Ranches of the Roaring Fork Valley were originally homesteaded to meet the demand for food and fodder (inset) in the silver-mining town of Aspen with its population approaching 15,000. After the silver crash of 1893, cattle, sheep, and potatoes replaced mining as the economic base of the region. (Denver Public Library, Western History Department) (Armstrong's journals)

Horse power

*C*harles Armstrong probably took this photograph of a young man on a hay sleigh. During winter months, a team of four strong horses provided the power to distribute hay to hungry cattle. (Amstrong's journals)

Unwelcome Gift, Mushrooms, Fire, and A Fine Parade

Thursday, May 30, 1901. Rainy. Geo. Besser went down on the stage. He has been over to Spring Creek. Miles Sweeney left a 1/2 pt of whiskey here on his way to town. It beats all. Now [that] I don't want the stuff, it seems every body is loaded with it, and wants me to drink.

Friday, May 31, 1901. Very rainy. Three men on the tramp stopped in out of the rain. They are going over to Taylor looking for work. I had a mess of mushrooms last night & some today.

Monday, July 1, 1901. The high water took out my footbridge while I was gone. The Tenderfoot Ranch house burned down last Monday and the people living there lost about everything they had. Frank Cunningham was in this afternoon on his way to Difficult Creek.

Thursday, July 4, 1901. I got up at 4.30 this morning. Walked to Aspen with Cap Green. They had a fine parade & there was lots of people in town. (Armstrong's journals)

Fencing them in

For generations Utes rode freely throughout the Roaring Fork Valley. Neither the Utes nor early prospectors could have imagined scrambling among a labyrinth of fences. Yet with cattle and sheep came barbed wire fencing. By the early 1900s, these strands of metal wire with barbs at regular intervals changed the face of Aspen, the Roaring Fork Valley, and the entire West. The bottom photograph features, from top to bottom, small sections of "Scutt's Rod and Rail" (patented October 23, 1883), "Brinkerhoff Ribbon" (patented May 17, 1881), and "Hodge's Parallel Rowell" (patented August 2, 1887). In the early days little love was lost, but lots of money was made, on barbed wire fencing. (Denver Public Library, Western History Department) (Author's collection)

142

Cowboys

With cattle came cowboys. Hollywood has instilled in the American public — and much of the world — a stereotype of the cowboy as a rugged, gun-toting, Indian-fighting individualist. Most men who tended to cattle in the Roaring Fork Valley did not carry guns, nor fight Indians, nor consider themselves rugged individualists. Rather, most of them worked long hours tending to the family ranching business. (Both from Crane, 1913)

The "Punch Bowl" on the Roaring Forks

A close view of water churning through a narrow passage in Roaring Fork Canyon between Aspen and Independence Pass appeared in a Colorado Midland Railway brochure. Combine this view with towering, snow-capped mountains and one understands why many Aspenites turned to tourism for economic salvation. (Denver Public Library, Western History Department)

144

"This place will appeal almost irresistably"

An early brochure touting Aspen's natural assets asserted: "To the lover of nature in her grander moods, this place will appeal almost irresistably [sic]. Majesty sits crowned upon the hills, and beneath them lies the ice-cold, silent, blue water in which millions of trout disport themselves. This is the favorite haunt for picnic parties and every summer sees scores of tourists from all over the United States camping here" (Aspen Commercial Club: undated).

Lower Maroon Lake, a popular camping and fishing spot, is shown above. South of Aspen, the picturesque Taylor Park region attracted many locals. A precocious ten-year-old Carl Gustaf Beck wrote a short essay reminiscing about his trip to Taylor Park and beyond (see next page). (Author's collection)

Gaunt Jacks, A Handout, and Daily Life

Tuesday, July 9, 1901. Walked up to Bob Long's Ranch and caught a fine brook trout. Found 3 of Bob Johnson's jacks in a cabin that had been there for a week or more. They were pretty gaunt. Gave a man his dinner, who said he had not had anything to eat since yesterday. So the day was not spent in vain. Harry Powers was up and got his pony. I had trout for supper.

Wednesday, July 10, 1901. Tried the fishing, no good. Busy all day. Got a grindstone from Fred's cabin. Heard a thunderstorm, but not much rain here. Took a walk down to Geo's cabin this evening.

Thursday, July 17, 1901. Hitched Dick to the cart and drove about 2 miles above Ashcroft and surveyed a tunnel for Charles OKane.

Thursday, July 24, 1901. I pulled out for home this morning. We have put in the time fishing & prospecting around, had fish every meal since we have been here. Yesterday we were up to Geo Besser's place. I got into camp on Taylor River at noon. Rained most of the afternoon, so I caught only one fish. (Armstrong's journals)

Our Camping Trip
Carl Gustaf Beck

In the summer of 1903 our family and another family started out on a camping trip up to Taylor Park. We had a nice trip, the road was fine and the scenery was beautiful. We came to a place named Horse-Shoe there we stopped and ate our dinner and enjoyed ourselves. Then came the range. We walked part of the way up. Finally we came to the top. There was lots of snow.

Before dark we came to Dorchester. There was an eating house, two stores and several houses which were used as bedrooms. We had a warm supper, and then went to bed in our cosy rooms. We were in Dorchester two days and nights. There we met some friends of ours that were out camping. Then we started for our camping place and it took us all day. We were nearly to a little town called Tin Cup. There in a big forest we put up our tents. We went down in a meadow where we caught grasshoppers and went fishing.

I caught my first fish while we were up there. Two friends of ours came up there. That night we told stories. We had a big camp fire to sit by. After two weeks we came home.

(Courtesy of the Beck family collection)

"Bridal Veil Falls — Ashcroft"

*T*he trail to Taylor Park took young Carl Beck through Ashcroft, now nearly a ghost town. Although it had lost its population, Ashcroft still retained its spectacular setting. To the east, just above the main settlement, Bridal Veil Falls flows above two log cabins. Today the falls is mostly obscured by tall stands of Aspen and pine. Someone in the Beck family wrote "Bridal Veil Falls — Ashcroft" beneath this photograph in an old family album. (Courtesy of Beck family collection)

146

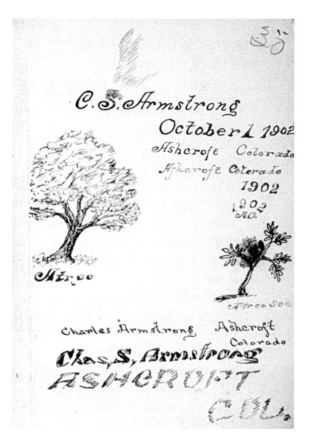

147

Armstrong in Ashcroft

After the turn of the century, Charles Armstrong continued to take frequent walks to Ashcroft (he lived a few miles north on Castle Creek) to visit a few close friends who remained. Armstrong and his Ashcroft compatriots often drank well into the night. As witnessed by drawings in his 1901 journal (left and center), Armstrong considered himself a resident of the nearly abandoned settlement. The art on the cover of his 1902 to 1905 journal (right) might indicate that he had a little more time on his hands. (Armstrong's journals)

148

Ashcroft luminaries

Dan McArthur, the "mayor" of Ashcroft and a close friend of Armstrong, Montezuma Mine superintendent Peter Larson, and miner George Crawford pose for the camera on the porch of the Ashcroft Post Office. Although "Ashcroft Post Office" is scribbled on the back of this photograph, the Blatz Beer sign suggests one could purchase more than stamps in this establishment. McArthur's cabin is shown below. (Colorado Historical Society, Stephen Hart Library) (Courtesy of Beck family collection)

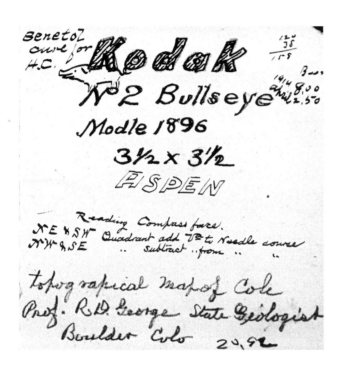

Armstrong's camera

*I*n the early 1900s Charles Armstrong purchased a Kodak camera (top). With it he captured several scenes in the Ashcroft and Aspen vicinity. Contrary to his tendency to record dates, names, and places, Armstrong labeled only two of over 100 photographs that came with his journals. This photograph shows what appears to be a small ranch above Ashcroft with Star Mountain in the background. (Both from Armstrong's journals)

A rare view

Seldom does one find an image of a cabin interior. This photograph in a Beck family album captures two men gambling in cramped quarters. Notice the candle burning in the window, photographs and posters covering the walls, and personal items resting on narrow shelves. Two beds take up most of the space. (Courtesy of the Beck family collection)

**Washing, Baking,
Dreams of A Railroad, and
President McKinley Assassinated**

Monday, July 29, 1901. I washed my duds & baked light bread. Very warm day. A party of R.R. surveyors are up Castle Creek & are going into Taylor Park with it. I met them at the Horseshoe last Saturday. The line is on the other side of the creek here. I hope they will build it. It will liven up this section & I may get some money yet.
Tuesday, August 6, 1901. I got up at 3 this morning. Was sick. Fainted once, & fell in the road.
Wednesday, August 7, 1901. Pete went to town on the stage. I shot 2 grouse this evening. The dog works fine hunting them up.
Friday, September 6, 1901. Mark Cunningham was in on his was to Difficult [Creek]. Had some budge [?] of course. McKinley shot today at Pan Amer. (Armstrong's journals)

151

Charles S. Armstrong?

*T*wo details suggest that this may be Charles S. Armstrong. First, this snapshot came with his journals. Second, Armstrong writes about his fancy buckskin jacket. On the other hand, this man appears younger than the 50 years that Armstrong would have been at the time. (Armstrong's journals)

152

Cold in Aspen

A postcard features a wintry and nearly deserted Hyman Avenue on March 16, 1906. Aspenites faced more than the harsh weather. The Colorado Midland Railroad declared bankruptcy. The price of silver hovered around a meager 71 cents per ounce. Wages at the Park Regent and Bushwacker Mines were cut to $2.50 per day. By 1908 only the Smuggler Mine remained open. (Courtesy of Joann Leech)

Pressure politics

During hard economic times political campaigns took on a more serious nature. Thus, the Republican headquarters (above) in Aspen attracted plenty of attention. Portraits of Republican presidential candidate William McKinley and running mate Theodore Roosevelt indicate who these men favored in the 1900 election. McKinley won, but on September 6, 1901, his presidency was cut short by an assassin's bullet. Roosevelt took his place and was re-elected as President in 1904. During this time he spearheaded the establishment of our now-cherished national park system. (Denver Public Library, Western History Department)

153

154

Roosevelt in Colorado

Teddy Roosevelt loved Colorado. His hunting and fishing expeditions to the Centennial state became the stuff of legend. Shown above is a Colorado Midland locomotive outfitted specially for Roosevelt, "Our President." He campaigned in Glenwood and Redstone.

In 1909 Roosevelt declined to run again. In 1912 supporters of Roosevelt wanted him back (top right), but his renegade Bull Moose party (bottom left) failed to carry him into office. (Colorado Historical Society, Stephen Hart Library) (Insets from author's collection)

Candlemas Day, Ground Hog Day, and Leadville Legend Dies

Sunday, February 2, 1902. Candlemas day, half your oats & half your hay. Ground hog day. Cloudy most of the time. Sun shone faintly part of forenoon. Neassnon [?] came up with his team. Had one passenger for Taylor Park. Dan sent down some Denver papers, one of which had the bad news of Abe Lee's death. He died of pneumonia last Thursday morning in Denver, & was buried Wednesday at 2 P.M. in Riverside Cemetery. They published his picture, a good likeness and a good account of his life. He was one of the 3 discoverers of California Gulch in 1859 [1860].

Monday, February 3, 1902. Splendid warm sunny day. I took a stroll as far as Hawkeye Cabin. Bad walking, but I enjoyed it first rate. Washed my duds & c. (Armstrong's journals)

Beck in Denver

Aspen's own Henry Beck, shown here at his desk in the state capitol, served in the House of Representatives in 1906. (Courtesy of the Beck family collection)

Baking Light Bread, Thousands Die, and Gambling for Beer

Thursday, May 15, 1902. Henry Powers brought his mare & colt up this morning. I baked light bread. We went fishing this evening. I caught 3 trout. Henry did not get any. I got a lb of coffee at Sebree's Cabin. I got a letter from him today. He broke his left arm some time ago.

Saturday, May 17, 1902. Wrote to George Sebree. Johnson went over Taylor Range with his jacks today, loaded with supplies for the Enterprise Mine. I sent up to Dan for a package of envelopes [for] 50c. He sent down a lot of papers with account of destruction of St. Perrie, with 30,000 inhabitants, by a volcano on the island of Martanique West Indias. Very windy & the air is full of dust.

Thursday, June 5, 1902. Stopped at Ashcroft on my way home & played several games of freeze out for the beer. Got stuck 40c. I had breakfast at 5.30 and had a tramp on hand for his morning meal. Quite a lot of fishermen along the creek.
(Armstrong's journals)

A cut above

These men are dressed better than most working Aspenites. They could be mine owners, businessmen, or both. Although this is probably in downtown Aspen, the precise location remains a mystery. (Armstrong's journals)

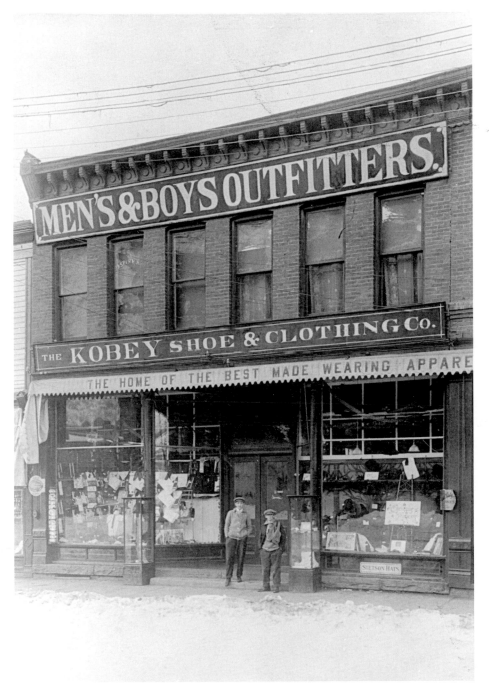

Kobey Shoe and Clothing Co.

157

*P*erhaps this popular Aspen clothing store provided the men in the previous photograph with their apparel. An ad for "Christmas Pictures" appears in the window. A "Stetson Hats" sign appears below the ad. (Colorado Historical Society, Stephen Hart Library)

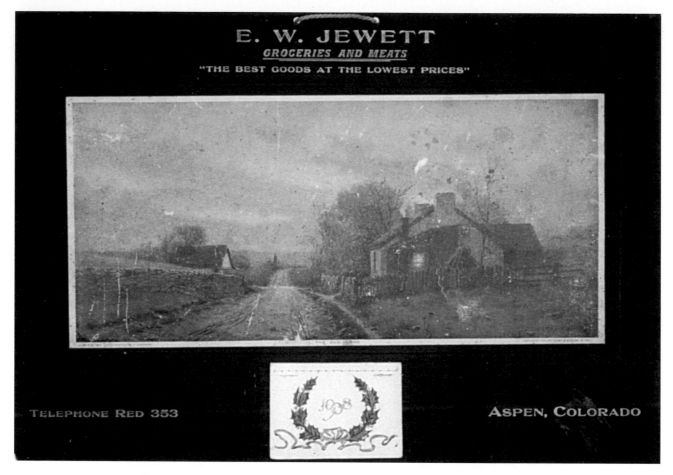

Life goes on in Aspen

By 1908 Aspen's population had plunged to fewer than 3,000. For those who remained, G. W. Jewett Groceries and Meats catered to their culinary needs. Eugene Wilder Jewett came to Aspen in 1888. He held interest in the Newman Mining, Milling, and Leasing Company, served as a member of the Aspen Board of Education for fourteen years, and represented Pitkin County in the Colorado State Legislature in 1923 - 1924. A 1908 calendar from Jewett's store on Galena Street is shown above. (Courtesy of Rick Sinner)

"The bike squad"

During this era bicycles and bicycle racing became very popular in the valley. Children loved to ride their bikes around town. Above, "The bike squad," as labeled in a Beck's family album, ready themselves to tear around the sunken bike circle (right). More serious riders entered the 20-mile race that paralleled the railroad grade from Basalt to Glenwood. Trains packed with fans shouted encouragement to their favorite riders. (Both courtesy of the Beck family collection)

Then came "automobile waggons"

No one in Aspen had seen anything quite like these noisy monstrosities. They frightened the horses and carved deep, dangerous ruts in dirt roads. Charles Armstrong was so impressed by what he saw on the streets of Aspen in the early 1900s that he drew a picture of these "automobile waggons" on the cover of his journal. Below the automobiles, a harness racer spurs on his steed. Notice, too, Armstrong's fine print beneath the "waggons" and the harness racer. He recorded the time it took each to cover one mile. (Armstrong's journals)

160

Speeders beware

Speeding automobile and motorcycle drivers became such a nusiance by the 1910s that Aspen had to threaten them with fines. A sign posted on the Castle Creek bridge reads: "Notice $25.00 fine . . . on this bridge . . . faster than . . . ."

John Zupancis (inset) poses proudly in the sidecar of his motorcycle. A friend grasps the handlebars of the powerful new machine. (Denver Public Library, Western History Department) (Courtesy of Adeline Zupancis Kirsten)

161

162

Downtown traffic

On the left two men show off their 1907 Stanley Steamer at the intersection of Mill Street and East Hyman Avenue. On the right two other men pose in a 1909 White Motor Company car. The Wheeler Opera House and Smuggler Mountain provide the backdrop for this intriguing image. In 1916 nearly 200 automobiles created confusion and dust problems throughout town. Yet no Aspenite could have known the profound affect that automobiles would ultimately have on the landscape of their city and the American way of life. (Denver Public Library, Western History Department)

Gambling Goes Under, Riding the Stage, Trapping Martin, and Long Snowshoes

Monday, December 8, 1902. I rode to Aspen with Charley. Got in to town at 1 oclock. I spent $6.35 in Post Office, orders for books &c. Got some things. In all, spent $14.85, but nothing foolishly. The Sheriff closed gambling in Aspen today. For good, I think.
Tuesday, December 9, 1902. I rode up on the stage this morning. Warm, fine day.
Wednesday, December 10, 1902. Fine. I was up the creek & set 5 traps for Martin. Gave John Berge 2 rabbits this evening.
Wednesday, December 17, 1902. Very fine. I went up above the Hawkeye to visit the traps. Found nothing. Took the long snow shoes & broke one., so I had to make the biggest part of the trip wading the snow. It was knee deep. I started the sweat good. (Armstrong's journals)

163

164

The last years of the Wheeler Opera House

Musicians, performers, and band members pose on the stage of the Wheeler Opera House. An elaborately decorated set includes muses, ornate paintings, scrolls, plants, pilasters, and arches. An orchestra pit can be seen in the foreground. Within a week in November 1912, two suspicious fires gutted the theatre of the once-proud edifice. The lower floors were still used for several years. (Denver Public Library, Western History Department)

165

Dreamland Theatre To-Night

A special program selected for this date and occasion

Edison Presents a Historical and Patriotic Drama, entitled—
"The Close of American Revolution"

Vitagraph presents a Big Comedy, entitled—
"The Man Higher Up"
Featuring John Bunny and Hugh Mach
Enough Said

Biograph Presents a Strong Drama, entitled—
"A Father's Lesson"
Don't Fail to See it

As a special attraction we have engaged the ever popular Wooden Shoe Artist—
Mr. Al Hogart (Happy)
Don't Fail to See the Pictures
Don't Fail to See the Dancing

The Dreamland Theatre

No match for the opulence of the Wheeler Opera House, the Dreamland Theatre could at least boast similar quality seats, since they salvaged them from the ashes of the opera house. In 1913 flickering "talkies" mesmerized Aspenites in the Dreamland and Isis Theatres.

On special occasions live performances (inset) took the Dreamland stage. Here a group of performers in front of the the Hotel Jerome drum up business for a "historical and patriotic drama." (Both from the Museum of Western Colorado)

166

No more whiskey jugs or tokens

Saloons owners who were able to stay open showed modest profits. During hard economic times more men turned to drink. Then in 1916 Colorado enacted prohibition. All the saloons closed their doors. And there were no more Aspen whiskey jugs or tokens like the ones shown above. That is not to say it was impossible to obtain spirits in the Roaring Fork Valley. (All courtesy of Rick Sinner)

Celebrating the Fourth of July

167

No matter how hard the times, most Aspenites turned out to enjoy the annual Fourth of July parades in grand style. Impressive floats like the one shown here thrilled crowds in downtown Aspen. (Aspen Historical Society)

168

"July 4, 1902"

Dressed in classic American regalia, a young Aspen girl and boy (Verner Beck) pose proudly for the camera. "July 4, 1902" is written on the back of this Kerwin and Gross photograph. (Courtesy of the Beck family collection)

Preparing for the parade

In 1910, a group of boys prepare to ride their burros — often called "Rocky Mountain canaries" — in Aspen's Fourth of July parade. (Denver Historical Society, Western History Department)

Labor Strife, The Price of Silver, and Hard Times in Montana

Saturday, March 21, 1903. SPRING BEGINS. Bill Ternsden [?] came up on the stage, bound for Taylor Park. Dan sent some papers. The miners in Cripple Creek struck in sympathy with the mills men at the Reduction Works at Colorado City.

Tuesday, April 28, 1903. Fine. Dan sent some papers. Silver is going up some. It is 51 1/2c now. I was up the creek early this morning looking at the traps, found nothing. Worked in the garden in afternoon.

Saturday, October 31, 1903. Fine day. I was up to Gent's pond with dog and gun, but saw nothing. Jackson & Milligan are doing assessment work on the Alpine Tunnel for Walter Clark. Dan sent some papers with the account of the shut down of the Copper Mines in Butte & Anaconda, letting out 15,000 miners. (Armstrong's journals)

169

170

Racing to the fire

Alvin Hogart led Aspen's championship hose cart team on Durant Avenue in 1907. He also served as an active member of the A. D. Hooper Hook and Ladder Company. Standing to the left is Fire Chief William Wack. The door to the Aspen fire house is open. A silver hose nozzle, one of several trophies captured by this crack crew, can be seen in the foreground.

Timed competitions among fire departments commanded the most attention during Fourth of July celebrations. These contests were more than entertainment. In the early twentieth century fire departments constituted sources of community pride and pillars of defense against the ever present danger of a cataclysmic fire. A city with a championship hose cart team could take comfort in knowing that they had the best fire protection possible. (Museum of Western Colorado) (Armstrong's journals)

Trapping Mink, Shipping Furs, and Digging Coal in Grand Junction

Friday, April 8, 1904. Very fine day., I was down the creek & set 3 traps for mink. I found one in one of the traps I had down there. But, a fox or coyote had dug it up & devoured 1/2 of it. I was in Sebree's cabin & got his hatchet & broom. Was up the creek & set 2 more traps. Was tired when I got home at 2.30. Fine crust to travel on. Thawing in afternoon.

Saturday, April 10, 1904. Walked up to Ashcroft early on the crust. Looked at the traps on the way, but found nothing. Shipped my furs, 3 mink & 1 martin, by mail to McMillan & Co. Minneapolis Minn. Spent 25c with Dan, & the postage was 25c. Coming home, I met Jack Leahy. He was [on] horseback going up home after samples. Lee stopped in here going back & had lunch & a good long talk. Lee has been digging coal the past winter in the Book Cliffs below Grand Junction. (Armstrong's journals)

"Eight Annual Ball, Thanksgiving Night, Nov 29, 1906"

For over two decades the Aspen Fire Department's Annual Balls proved to be one of the highlights of the social season. (Museum of Western History)

EIGHTH ANNUAL BALL
ASPEN FIRE DEPARTMENT
FRATERNAL HALL   THANKSGIVING NIGHT, NOV. 29, 1906

171

172

More than a sport

Aspen took pride in its hose cart teams. It lived and died by its baseball teams. By the summer of 1881, Aspen, Ashcroft, and Independence already boasted organized teams. In the early years the games gained a reputation for attracting rowdy crowds who craved bragging rights. Shown above is the Aspen Baseball Club. (Museum of Western Colorado)

Local hero

*I*n the early 1900s, Alvin Hogart (left) did more than lead Aspen's championship hose cart team. He excelled in baseball as well. The archival narrative accompanying this image read: "At bat 100 times — 54 hits — played first base, pitcher. batting av. 528." (Museum of Western Colorado)

173

Elk on rails

*E*lk disembarking from a railroad cattle car is not an everyday sight. Yet in 1913 that is exactly what people witnessed in Aspen. The Elks Lodge paid for shipping elk from Idaho to the Crystal City in hope of replenishing depleted elk herds. This group of elk was released at the head of Hunter Creek. The motivation for this was commercial. If local elk herds increased, more hunters would come and more money would flow into Aspen's depleted coffers. Charles Armstrong made note of this unusual occurrence in one of his journals, the cover of which is shown left. (Aspen Historical Society).

174

HISTORIC ASPEN IN RARE PHOTOGRAPHS

A hunter's paradise

*I*n the latter half of the nineteenth century, tourists and residents called Colorado a hunter's paradise. By the 1910s, overzealous hunters (shown here) had decimated Colorado's big-game populations. (Both from Crane, 1913)

176

One dollar fishing and hunting license

A faded and discolored photograph still bears witness to a successful fishing excursion by Aspen's Zupancis family. John Zupancis's 1917 Colorado fishing and hunting license (right) cost one dollar.

During this halcyon era, trains dropped fishermen at their favorite river spot and picked them up at their leisure. (Courtesy of Adeline Zupancis Kirsten)

Interior of the Aspen Post Office

Aspen postal workers look at the photographer in January 1915. Not much mail passed through this old post office located in the Independence Building on the southeast corner of Cooper Avenue and Galena Street. On the back of the photograph someone wrote: "Left to right Mary Kalmes, George Rohrbough [postmaster] Edna Cole [Mrs. Ray Eperson] and Chas. Hyatt." Visible in this image is a 1915 calendar, a large mail gurney, mail boxes, typewriter, and a postal counter.

On January 29, 1918, the Aspen Post Office handled John Zupancis's draft notice (inset). (Denver Public Library, Western History Department) (Courtesy of Adeline Zupancis Kirsten)

177

178

Chasing Francisco ("Pancho") Villa

*A*spenite John Zupancis (left) served in Nogales, Arizona (right). For his participation in the "Mexican Raids" he received the Mexican service medal shown above. (All courtesy of Adeline Zupancis Kirsten)

AMERICAN RAIDS INTO MEXICO ARE TOLD OF

[By Associated Press.]

El Paso, Tex., Aug. 28.—The recent United States military expedition after bandits penetrated farther into Mexican territory than any since the punitive expedition which was sent across the border under General John J. Pershing on March 15, 1916, in pursuit of Francisco Villa's bandit band.

That expedition, which followed the Villa raid on Columbus, N. M., in which seventeen persons were killed, was composed of 4,000 men, who marched more than 200 miles into the territory of the southern republic.

On several other occasions in the past two years, small detachments of troops have been sent across the border in pursuit of marauding bands. On August 27, 1918, American and Mexican troops fought two hours at Nogales, Ariz. The Mexican losses were 119 killed.

During the attack of Villa forces on Juarez, Brigadier General James B. Erwin, on June 15th last, ordered 3,600 United States troops to cross from El Paso, Tex., to prevent firing from the Mexican side into this city.

Yourself and Lady are Cordially invited
to attend a
Welcome Home Banquet and Dance
for Our Returned
Soldiers and Sailors
at Jerome Hotel
Saturday Evening, August 23, 1919
Banquet 7:30, Jerome Hotel   Dancing 9, Fraternal Hall

Tuesday Nov 11th
Armistice day. Everybody celebrating by
ringing of bells, blowing of whistles &
firing guns &c. Fair day.

Off to World War I

Before marching off to a monstrously bloody war in Europe, a group of young men are given a rousing sendoff at the Denver and Rio Grande Railroad depot in Aspen. Pinned to their lapels are ribbons inscribed with, "National Army, Pitkin County, Colorado" (left). Those who returned home received a "Welcome Home Banquet and Dance" at the Hotel Jerome on August 23, 1919 (top right). (Left, center, and top right all courtesy of Adeline Zupancis Kirsten) (Bottom right from Armstrong's journals)

Still mining ore

During the 1910s a few mines in the Aspen region reopened and reported fair to good lead, zinc, and silver ores. Above, the Smuggler Mine and Mill (possibly the zinc mill) continued to operate as well, although it showed only marginal profits. Water proved to be the nemesis of most mines. Without a good pumping system, shafts quickly filled with the troublesome liquid. (Armstrong's journals)

Killing Sheep, A Kodak Camera, 30,000 Trout, and Roosevelt Wins

Saturday, July 9, 1904. The cattle men held up the sheep men in Taylor Park Thursday and killed 600 or 800 sheep. Frank Stewart was in & got a cup of coffee on his way to town.

Wednesday, July 20, 1904. Fished all day. I caught 40. Was over to where the cattle men killed the sheep. There were 2 or 3 hundred killed, instead of 1,500 as was reported.

Saturday, August 20, 1904. We took a number of pictures with a Kodak of Charles cabin, claims, & c.. I was hunting for woodchuck, but did not get any.

Monday, August 22, 1904. We drove to town. I got home about 5.30. Spent $1.00 for meat & c.. Saw an old timer that used to be up Conundrum. His name is Swartz. Harold Clark & Porter Nelson put 30,000 trout in Castle Creek above the Tenderfoot Ranch this evening.

Tuesday, August 23, 1904. At home all day. Made out the certificates on the Highball Lodes for Dan McArthur & sent them up by the stage. Caught fine lot of trout & gave them to Henry Beck. He gave me some Bug juice. Frank OHirel [?] was here. He was fishing I lent some bacon to Charles Elithorpe [?]. Got letter from Sebree offering $75.00 for Henry Power's mare & colt. I answered it, accepting the offer.

Friday, September 19, 1904. Caught a mink this morning, but the skins are not good yet.. Baked bread & stewed the fruit I got yesterday. Wrote a letter to Henry Weber at Vernal Utah inquiring about the Unita Reservation & the country in general.

Tuesday, September 20, 1904. Fixing up the cart & outfit. Charles Torry & George Brum stopped in & ate their lunch on their way to Difficult Camp. Rained some in the evening.

Thursday, November 10, 1904. Roosevelt swept the country. I turned over my county warrant to Johnson & Bonnell, $15.00. Got home 4 a.m. Thermometer 6 below. Very cold. To bring me luck I voted for a winner this time.

Plow deep while sluggards sleep And you will have corn to sell and keep. Poor Richard. Froze potatoes in wood shed.

Tuesday, May 30, 1905. Declaration day I never thought of it, or I would have gone to town as they are going to have quite a celebration. I was up to Fred Griswold's tunnel & got some boards for a sluice for my irrigation ditch. Mr Burnside gave me an Aspen Times with the news that Japs have annihilated the Great Russian fleet in the Korean Straits. Jack Leahy went down on the stage. Says he is going to Grand Junction. Dan sent papers. I planted some seeds in my new garden. Creek booming this evening.

Tuesday, June 1, 1905. I walked up to Ashcroft. Tried the fishing with no luck. Had dinner with Miles Sweeney. Pete Olson & a lot more people went over Taylor Range. He is going to start a saloon at Dorchester. (Armstrong's journals)

181

Deep-sea divers in Aspen

*I*n 1910 the Smuggler Mine hired professional deep-sea divers to repair a large broken pump submerged under forty-five feet of water in one of the shafts. David Hyman, among others, believed that richer ore could be found deeper in the mine. After several days of strategy sessions and hard, dangerous work the divers successfully repaired the pump. Aspen newspapers used a lot of ink detailing the daring exploits of the divers. (Aspen Historical Society)

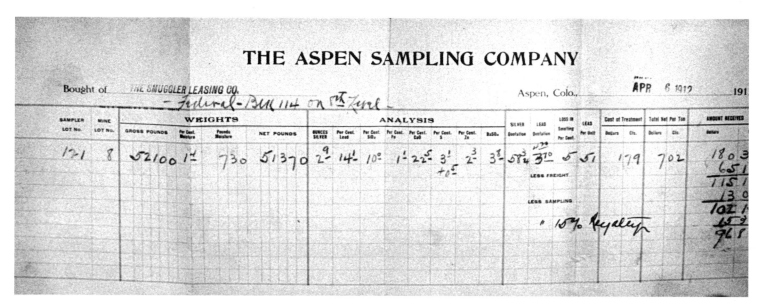

Ore samples

he few mines that remained open frequently sent ore samples to The Aspen Sampling Company, hoping for rich assay reports. An assay receipt for The Smuggler Leasing Company is shown here, along with a small paper ore-sample bag. (Both courtesy of Ben Kirsten)

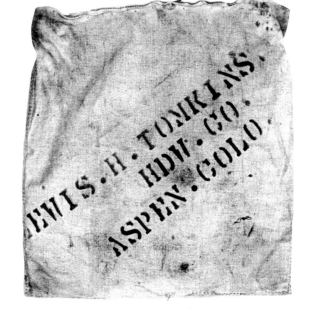

Specialized ore bags

Some Aspen mining companies shipped their high-quality ores to other cities for processing. For those that did, Tomkins Hardware sold them specially marked ore bags (shown here). The "A. S & R. Co." stenciled on this bag stands for the Argo Smelting and Refining Company that once stood near Denver in Globeville. (Both courtesy of Ben Kirsten)

Coroner's Jury, Difficult Creek Camp, Whoppers, and San Francisco Earthquake

Wednesday, July 5, 1905. Got $75⁰⁰ off Charles Keyser to pay for surveying that he wants done. I paid Johnson Bonnell & Co $50⁰⁰. I was on the coroner's jury over an Austrian that was killed yesterday in a fight. Had his skull fractured by a rock thrown by another Austrian. I rode Jack Leahy's horse home. Got here about 9.30pm.
Friday, July 7, 1905. Ther. 42 at 7.30am. Charles Shriver was in this morning on his way up to Difficult Creek Camp. I caught 3 trout for dinner.
Monday, July 31, 1905. Baked bread. Caught a mess of fish. Saw Dave Brown & Jack Atkinson. They have been fishing in the lake on Taylor Range. They caught 22 whoppers. They were the biggest Brook trout I ever saw. Would weigh 3 or 4 lbs cleaned. I must get up there & try my luck.
Wednesday, November 22, 1905. Attended the Farmer's Institute all day. It was good. The professors from the State Agricultural College were the speakers.
Thursday, April 19, 1906. Earth Quake in San Fransesco yesterday morning. Destroyed much of the city. (Armstrong's journals)

Lewis H. Tomkins Hardware Company

*L*ocated on the corner of Cooper Avenue and Galena Street, the Lewis H. Tomkins store began selling hardware goods in Aspen in the 1880s. A souvenir dish and a 1912 receipt from the venerable store are shown here. (Courtesy of Ben Kirsten) (Courtesy of Leo Stambaugh)

186

Fragile souvenirs

During the first two decades of the twentieth century, local merchants continued to sell tourists mining-related souvenirs. A fragile china cream pitcher featuring an idealized drawing of "The Silver Smuggler and The Mollie Gibson Mines" survives to this day. Aspen historian Larry Fredrick notes that no one ever added "Silver" to the Smuggler name, and that the shaft house shown on the pitcher is the Free Silver shaft house that burned in 1897. (Courtesy of Leo Stambaugh)

"Enterprise Flyer — 1910"

*T*hese Aspen miners never saw the glory days. A mule is chained to the ore carts. All ore carts, even during the boom, were either pushed by men or pulled by mules. (Courtesy of the Beck family collection)

Adorned with posters

*T*he top image carries the handwritten caption: "My Bunk at the Star." It is a rare interior view of an Aspen miner's modest quarters. Leather boots tilt in the left foreground. Theatrical posters of attractive young women surround a fish identification chart. By the bed a hand-pump shotgun leans again the wall. Right, a group of miners pose for the camera in similarly decorated quarters. (Both courtesy of the Beck family collection)

Touring the mines

*L*ocals and tourists loved to tour the mines. Consequently, a few mine owners supplemented their income with mine tours. More often, mine owners gave free tours to potential investors and new school teachers. Here a group of men and women who are about to go down into the Durant Mine stand in front of a wood-frame house. Several of the men wear miners' candles stuck through their hatbands. The man squatting in front points his camera at the photographer. (Denver Public Library, Western History Department)

B. Clark Wheeler, Opera House, Mining Suffers, and 20 Years for Murder

Tuesday, October 1, 1907. Fine day. Surveying on Famous Ditch finished levels B. Clark Wheeler was up to see us.

Thursday, October 3, 1907. Walked to town. Went to the fair in afternoon. Very good display and a good attendance. Went to the Opera House this evening to a free concert by the Redstone band, and they gave a fine entertainment. Cold yesterday.

Friday, November 29, 1907. I am 60 years old today. Am in good health & would like to get in 60 more years and see what the world would accomplish.

Friday, December 13, 1907. Stormy. I put in the day cooking & washing. I hear that the Montezuma has shut down.

Friday, December 20, 1907. I was visiting John R. Mason this afternoon. Did not go down-town. The Smuggler Mine laid off 200 men this evening.

Friday, April 24, 1908. Snowing. Washed my duds & c. John Taylor hung himself last night in the jail at Glenwood. He was sentenced to 20 years in prison for killing his wife. (Armstrong's journals)

190

409A   Water Falls in Durant Mine, Aspen, Colo., 1 mile under ground

Deep in the Durant

One mile underground this "Water Falls in Durant Mine" pleased curiosity seekers, but not miners. Throughout Aspen's history, the specter of water-filled mines haunted all the miners' and mine owners' dreams. (Courtesy of Beck family collection)

Unloading timber at the Smuggler

A wagon driver readies to unload his cargo of timber at the Smuggler mining complex. The cut timber probably rolled down the two large logs into a sawmill. In 1918 Smuggler miners went on strike, but they could not hold out for long. Too many miners were looking for work, any work.

Approximate "production figures to date [1918]" for major mining areas in the Aspen region: Smuggler Mountain ($50,000,000), Aspen Mountain ($49,250,000), Tourtelotte Park ($4,000,000), Richmond Hill ($1,500,00), and Lenado ($250,000). (Armstrong's journals)

Titanic Sinks, Fish Hooks, Governor Speaks, and Death

Monday, April 22, 1912. Walked to town. The past week has been stormy & bad so I did not get out much. Rustled wood was about all I did. The papers are full of the loss of the steamer Titanic off New Foundland. Last Monday morning [it] ran into an iceberg & sunk. About 1,600 people lost.

Thursday, May 2, 1912. I got home 1 oclock this morning. Was up town today. Spent 10c for fish hooks & 10c for weinerwurst Was up town this evening. Lost 20c playing cards.

Thursday, July 4, 1912. Quite a celebration. Governor Shafroth spoke in the evening in the Opera House. After the speech there was a free picture show. Very cold, disagreeable day.

Monday, July 29, 1912. Mox Snyder was found dead in Jake Reikert's cabin above Ashcroft yesterday. Well Mox has wanted to die for a long time & now has his wish. All things come to those that wait. Mr. Cooper, the Grand Lecturer of Colo. A.F. & A. M., lectured at Masonic Hall this evening. Very good. I gave H. Koch the plat of the fish ponds this evening. (Armstrong's journals)

192

Mining marble

Due west of North Maroon Peak above Snowmass, not far from Aspen as the crow flies, men mined marble. The world-famous Yule Marble Company quarry is shown above in about 1914. Rising from the power house, a crane towers over the workers. A large block of marble swings from the end of the crane cable. It will be attached to the mechanism hanging from the even larger cables, then transported down to the shipping area. (Denver Public Library, Western History Department)

Marble for the Lincoln Memorial

A striking bird's-eye view of the Yule Marble Company plant in Marble is shown above. Inside the long building are diamond saws, gang saws, and rubbing beds. A separate building constructed solely for preparing marble for the Lincoln Memorial in Washington, D.C. can be seen by the back right of the plant. Shown, too, are the shipping and receiving areas, the Crystal River, and San Juan Railroad rolling stock. The facility closed in 1941.

Below the quarry, Marble citizens inherited Aspen's small Episcopalian Church that once stood on Bleeker Street. (Denver Public Library, Western History Department) (Courtesy of Adeline Zupancis Kirsten)

194

Redstone "Castle"

A few miles north of Marble along Crystal River stood Redstone, named after the cliffs above it. In this company town, profits from coke production around the turn of the twentieth century helped build a "castle of redstone" for John Cleveland Osgood. Osgood called his home "Cleveholm." With the decline of mining and smelting in Colorado, demand for coke fell precipitously. By 1909, Redstone was no more. The stately castle, however, remains as a monument to this brief, prosperous era. (Courtesy of Ben Kirsten)

Washington School

Built in 1890, the venerable three-story Washington School received students well into the twentieth century. The school has a bell-shaped roof, dormer and rectangular windows, several chimneys, and a cupola. It was condemned in 1941. (Courtesy of Adeline Zupancis Kirsten)

"A letter to Miss Sanders, Aspen, Colo., Mar. 4, 1909."

Dear Miss Sanders,

I am sorry that I did not get to say good-bye when you left. I am well now and am going to school. I like our new teacher very much but I miss you.

The diphtheria is coming in town now and we all have to bring our own drinking cups.

There is one case here we are sure of and there are more that we are not sure of.

I wish I was in California with you, where the grass and trees are green and where we can have fresh oranges.

The snow is up to my knees. It is snowing now but it is rather warm.

All the children that were out on account of the measles are back now. We are getting along fine in Arithmetic and Geography. We are going to have a test in spelling Monday, and the A class is going to have one Friday.

The A class had a test in History and Arithmetic last Monday. They did well.

Your pupil
Carl Beck. (right)

(Courtesy of Beck family collection)

Eighth-grade graduating class

*O*n May 30, 1910, Washington School's eighth-grade graduating class pose in front of the brick and sandstone building. The girls are dressed in white, long-sleeved shirts with high collars and puffed sleeves. Several of the girls wear corsages, and many have large bows behind their heads. The boys wear breeches, jackets, shirts, bow ties, and leather shoes. Several of the boys in the front row have their arms around one another. (Denver Historical Society, Western History Department)

Working for Wheeler, Surveying, and Smuggler Miners on Strike

Sunday, October 13, 1912. Walked to Aspen. Stopped a short time at the Famous Tunnel. Took dinner with Bill Robinson & Willis Mead. They are building fence at Highland for B. Clark Wheeler. Muddy roads making hard walking. Got to town about 5 P.M.

Monday, October 14, 1912. Fine weather. Called on John R. this evening. Had a few drinks.

Tuesday, October 15, 1912. Surveyed a claim for the Hope Mining Co. Took dinner at the Little Annie Mine. Got home 7 P.M.

Wednesday, October 16, 1912. Fine weather. All the men on the Smuggler Mine are on strike. They won't work under the Boss whose name is Hoar. They say he is a driver & no good. Teddy Roosevelt was shoot by a crank, day before yesterday at Milwaukee. Not dangerously hurt.

(Armstrong's journals)

197

Tennis court at Lincoln School

Mrs. Lola Adams stands on the Lincoln School tennis court holding a racket above her head. Behind her, the clapboard L-shaped school has a gabled and hipped roof. A cupola rises above the entrance. Lincoln School was condemned in 1927. (Denver Public Library, Western History Department)

From home to high school

Silver baron D. C. R. Brown (inset) built this mansion in the late 1880s. The two-story masonry building features a gabled roof, eyelid dormer, and a large turret with a bell-shaped roof and embrocated brickwork. The structure has rectangular and arched windows, as well as a gabled front porch with spindles. After the turn of the century, Brown generously donated his mansion to the city to serve as Aspen's only high school.

D. C. R. Brown — unlike Henry P. Gillespie, B. Clark Wheeler, and Jerome Wheeler — diversified his business interests in Aspen and died a millionaire. (Denver Historical Society, Western History Department)

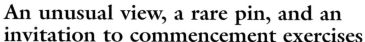

An unusual view, a rare pin, and an invitation to commencement exercises

Why Charles Armstrong kept a photograph of the backside of Aspen High School remains a mystery. The Aspen High School pin (inset) is silver. An invitation to the 1918 Aspen High School Commencement Exercises at the First Presbyterian Church is also shown (right). (Armstrong's journals) (Courtesy of Ed Borasio) (Courtesy of Adeline Zupancis Kirsten)

Aspen High School

Commencement Exercises

on Thursday evening, May the twenty-third

nineteen hundred and eighteen

at Presbyterian Church, eight o'clock

Aspen, Colorado

Football team, 1909

High school football games ranked high on the social scale in most mining towns, including Aspen. Here team members crouch in an offensive alignment on the Aspen High School playing field. They are wearing long-sleeved practice shirts, padded pants, and high-topped football shoes typical of the time. One hopes they donned leather helmets once the photographer left. (Denver Public Library, Western History Department)

201

Venison Steak, Picture Show, and Ptomaine Poison

Saturday, October 19, 1912. Andy Park came in from the Enterprise Mine yesterday. I was around with him today. He has quit for the winter.

Sunday, October 20, 1912. Was over to the hospital with Andy to see Bill Dickerson. I took supper with Andy this evening. Had venison stake [sic]. It was fine. Wrote to Charles Rausch about claim.

Tuesday, October 22, 1912. Went to the picture show this evening with Andy Park. It was good. Got $2.00 worth of coal.

Friday, October 25, 1912. Fine weather we are having, but cold nights. Quite a severe Earth-quake at 20 minutes to 11 AM. Bert Canning died in Salida Hospital yesterday from ptomaine poison, from eating sourkrout & weinerwourst.

(Armstrong's journals)

202

Girls basketball team, 1910

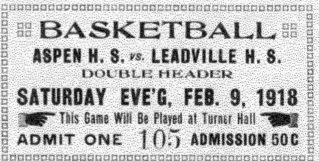

Properly attired in Victorian dress, young ladies of the Aspen girls basketball team pose for a team picture on the steps of a hotel in Buena Vista, Colorado. Their luggage is lined up in front of the steps. All the team members wear broad-brimmed hats. A row of men, whose heads are not visible, stand on the top step behind the seated women.

A 1918 ticket for a "double header" basketball game between Aspen and Leadville is also shown. (Denver Public Library, Western History Department) (Courtesy of Gary Bracken)

Symbols of success

*I*n 1911 a young Lola Adams shades the sun's rays from her eyes as she gazes at the camera over trophies won by Aspen High School athletic teams. (Denver Public Library, Western History Department)

204

Men, boys, burros, and a wagon

Men and boys wearing overalls pose in front of the Irving Adams house in 1910. Whatever the occasion for this gathering, the boy on the lead burro does not seem enthusiastic about it. (Denver Public Library, Western History Department)

Bucking a calf

Charles Armstrong had this photograph of a young boy bucking a calf. A star shows on the saddle blanket. A calf was not easy to ride because it could easily wiggle the saddle down over its head. (Armstrong's journals)

Surveying, Getting Drunk, Opera House Fire, and a 65th Birthday

Sunday, November 11, 1912. Rained in the night & snowed most of the day. I packed my bed over to the Forest office this morning to go up to work on the road. But they did not go. Got a letter from Charles Boyd at Grand Junction. He says times are good there.

Tuesday, November 12, 1912. Got $10⁰⁰ off Thatcher on account. I charged him $15⁰⁰ for surveying. I got drunk this evening. Went to the picture show. After the show, the Opera House caught afire on the stage. Did about $1,000 damage.

Thursday, November 21, 1912. Rode up to the cabin on the stage. John Robinson went up to his place. The roads are fine. No snow or mud. I was to the Opera House fire about 2.30 this morning. It gutted the stage & most of the upper part & did a lot of damage to the store on the ground floor by water.

Friday, November 29, 1912. I am 65 years old today. And I got drunk & spent $5⁰⁰. (Armstrong's journals)

206

Traveling bear

Another Armstrong photograph focuses on a bear surrounded by a group of men and a boy. Behind the man wearing the light-colored suspenders, a horse warily eyes the beast. For a few years someone in Aspen kept a bear at the Clarendon Hotel. Most likely, however, this was a "dancing," or "trained" bear traveling with its owner through Aspen. Some trained bears actually fought local boxers. (Armstrong journals)

From Ashcroft to Aspen

During the first two decades of the twentieth century, people "freighted," meaning moved, several small homes from Ashcroft to Aspen. Here Armstrong photographed a man driving a horse, most likely in an attempt to align properly a house that once stood in Ashcroft. By 1919 Aspen had fewer than 1,500 residents. According to the Colorado State Business Directory, Ashcroft, and Independence had none. (Armstrong's journals)

207

Unknown lodgings

An elderly, mustached man sits in a chair with his faithful dog by his side. The exact location of the old hewn-log bunkhouse is unknown, although it could have been built by Charles Armstrong. In his 1880s and 1890s journals he frequently wrote about having "boarders" at his place above Highland on Castle Creek. In fact, this could be Armstrong in his later years posing in front of his boarding place. (Armstrong's journals)

Two girls on a swing

*L*illi and Mimmie Hogart sit on a swing in their backyard. This austere, drab scene on the "working" end of town — the East End, does not mesh with Aspen's prosperous image, either then or now. (Museum of Western Colorado)

Girl in a fountain

*T*his picture fits the Aspen stereotype. A young Lola Adams sits in the center of a dry circular fountain in front of Aspen High School which was once D. C. R. Brown's house. She wears a long coat, bloomers, leather shoes, and a bonnet tied under her chin. Behind her, there is a statue of a boy holding an umbrella over himself and a petite girl. (Denver Public Library, Western History Department)

209

Female Friends, Still Drinking, Elk Ride the Train, and Frigid Weather

Friday, March 14, 1913. Cold & stormy. Jack Leahy was here this evening with a lot of good lunch. We called on Cora May & Mrs Magee and had a good visit.

Saturday, March 15, 1913. I put in most of the day roping trunks & c for Cora & Minnie. Saw them off on the D&R.G. at 5 P.M. Cora & Helen for Goldfield & Mrs. Magee for Montrose. I moved part of my stuff to Cora's house.

Sunday, March 16, 1913. I slept in the Johnson house last night. Called on John R with 1/2 pint. After we got away with that, we walked over to Tagart's ranch to see [the] elk. Twenty of them came in on the morning train. The Forest service brought them in and are going to turn them onto the range. After we came home, John R. helped me move some of my stuff over here. Very cold nights. But fine day today. (Armstrong's journals)

Fashionable bisque doll

A self-assured young girl poses with a fashionable bisque doll amidst opulent accoutrements. (Armstrong's journals)

210

Confident pose

A well-dressed Aspen boy sporting a watch and chain strikes a confident pose. "John Simpson" is written on the back of this photograph. (Museum of Western Colorado)

Pioneer Park

*I*n 1909 several women dressed in winter coats and hats gather near snowy Pioneer Park. Today one can still stroll by Aspen's Pioneer Park on Bleeker Street. (Denver Public Library, Western History Department)

212

S. S. Lusitania Sinks, County Roads, Cabbage Plants, and Baseball

Saturday, May 8, 1915. Fine day. The news is the sinking of the S.S. Lusitania, with the loss of 1,300 passengers. It was torpedoed by German Submarines off the coast of Ireland.
Saturday, May 22, 1915. Rode down to town this evening with Courtney. Got here about 6 oclock. I tried the fishing this afternoon with no success. I did 5 days work on the road for the county while I was up here. Last week was very stormy & I did nothing much but sit in the cabin & read old magazines. Caught one rabbit & made a good stew.
Wednesday, May 25, 1915. At home all day. Rainy. I got some cabbage plants off Harold Clark. Set out some this afternoon. Was up this AM at 3.45 and rustled some wood. Very rainy afternoon & evening. Sunday, June 20, 1915. Was over to the ball grounds with Park to see the game between the Basalt & Aspen clubs. Aspen 20 Basalt 4. (Armstrong's journals)

The Pleasure Seeker's Club

What Aspen lacked in size it often made up in enthusiasm. Here local women in the Pleasure Seeker's Club are most likely planning their next activity. Picnics in alpine meadows often ranked high on their agenda. Antique furniture connoisseurs will have a hard time keeping their eyes off the wooden rectangular table with thick, carved legs. (Denver Public Library, Western History Department)

Enjoying the alpine environment

*I*n 1909 two women and two young girls in a open carriage enjoy a ride into Aspen's countryside. Most likely this is the "summer road" up Shadow Mountain. (Denver Public Library, Western History Department)

Pearl Pass trip

To reach Pearl Pass this group had to ride about fifteen miles south from Aspen, up through Highland and Ashcroft. Once on top of the pass they were rewarded with some of the most spectacular mountain views in Colorado. The women may be members of the Pleasure Seeker's Club. (Denver Public Library, Western History Department)

Montgomery Ward Gun, A Deadly Accident, Tungsten, and the Price of Silver

Tuesday, August 17, 1915. Sent $5.66 to Montgomery Ward for a gun & ammunition. Pd $1.00 for hunting lisence, 75 cts for grub.

Thursday, August 19, 1915. Bad accident up at the Hope Tunnel. Ted Cooper, Arthur Demaris, & 2 girls went in the tunnel last night & were overcome with gas and did not get out till this morning. Young Demaris was dead & Cooper nearly so, & the two girls were unconscious. The 3 will pull through. I was up to the courthouse cooking up some claims for Mr. MacKenzie from Ashcroft. I don't know if I will get anything for it or not.

Saturday, April 29, 1916. Have been busy the past week planting garden & c. Yesterday was up the Roaring Fork in the granite, prospecting for tungsten, but found none. Silver is 73 1/4c today, the highest since the panic of 93. Charles MacBride died yesterday. Storming all day today. About 6 inches of snow this evening. Frank Green & Pete Olson went up to Ashcroft today. I ground up a nice lot of horseradish this morning. Phil Crosby was here visiting all the afternoon. (Armstrong's journals)

215

Picnicking above timberline

On their way to the top of Pearl Pass this group stopped for lunch above timberline. Patches of snow cover the tundra. (Denver Public Library, Western History Department)

HISTORIC ASPEN IN RARE PHOTOGRAPHS

Smiling in the high country

Every Aspenite, it seems, smiled in the high country. Here "Edith, Elin Beck, and a friend" smile wide grins for the photographer. Elin Beck (center) holds the barrel of a breech-loading rifle. Her friend grasps a smaller caliber pump. One wonders what they were hunting. (Courtesy of Beck family collection)

"Camp Stove, Hen Roost 1913"

Once again girls in a Beck family album smile at the camera, this time by their camp stove during a high-country outing. (Courtesy of the Beck family collection)

Aspen Block Burns, A 72nd Birthday, Mesa Store, and A Snowshoe Rabbit

Thursday, November 27, 1919. Thanksgiving. About 3 feet of new snow. Big fire up town last evening. The Aspen block burned. The Aspen drug store, Beals furniture store, & The Three Rules clothing store burned out. I was home all day. Park called & told me about the fire.

Saturday, November 29, 1919. I am 72 years old today. Was up town & got the mail. Read post card from Roxie. She is well. Stormy & cold. Jack Leahy here this evening till 10. I pd $2.00 to the Humdinger.

Tuesday, December 2, 1919. Fine, sunny. Washed my duds. Bought $1.10 grub at Mesa Store. 1# coffee for 50c,. & soupbone for 25c., and apples 25c., cough drops 10c. John Hawthorn came down from the Oakland. Jack Leahy called this evening.

Saturday, December 6, 1919. About 3 inches of new snow. Stormy day. I caught a snowshoe rabbit in a snair last night. Got $1.15 grub at Mesa Store. (Armstrong's journals)

"On top of the world"

*I*n about 1919, John Zupancis and Joe Bishop stand "on top of the world [possibly Mt. Elbert], looking toward Independence 3 miles away." Aspen, of course, was no longer on top of the world. Few people who witnessed the boom years of the 1880s and early 1890s could have envisioned the beleaguered Aspen of the 1900s and 1910s. In the 1920s, things would get even worse. (Courtesy of Adeline Zupancis Kirsten)

HISTORIC ASPEN IN RARE PHOTOGRAPHS

CHAPTER FOUR
Skiing and High Culture (1920s-1940s)

As the 1920s dawned, few could find reason to be optimistic about Aspen's economic future. The population dwindled steadily. Most mines closed. Nor did it help that in 1920 the Colorado Midland Railway, an early benefactor of the Crystal City, dismantled its line into the once-proud city. A sense of pending doom began to settle over the city. In winter snow fell on nearly deserted downtown streets. High above Aspen, chilly winds whistled through Ashcroft's abandoned buildings. In summer, a few tourists still brought money to town, but it did not amount to much and few people benefited. During prohibition, bootlegging supplemented Aspenites' incomes, as arrest records of the early 1920s attest. Come 1926, the Aspen Smelting Company, a pillar of the economy, suspended operations and the *Aspen Daily Times* became a weekly newspaper for the first time since 1885. On May 8, 1926, Charles S. Armstrong, with trembling hand, scribbled the last entry into his diary, poignantly ending an extraordinary personal record spanning fifty-nine years. (I often wonder what Armstrong would write in his journal if he could see Aspen now.)

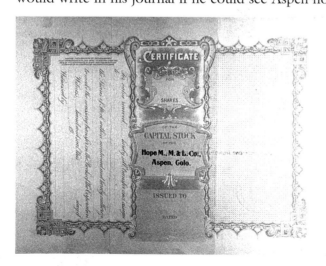

Yet in the face of seemingly insurmountable odds, the Crystal City simply refused to die. The suitably named Hope Mine continued to operate despite the low price of silver. In 1920, the Park Company Mine discovered a six-foot vein of ore, bearing potentially profitable amounts of silver. Fiscal faith in this discovery resulted in the construction of a 7,000-foot tram to transport the silver-rich ore down Aspen Mountain. Aspen's first flower show blossomed in 1921. More importantly, citizens continued to work on making the Independence Pass road fit for automobile travel. Within three years they were rewarded with the sight of cars rambling over the spectacular summit of the pass, at least during the summer months. The increasing popularity of automobiles also caused problems. In 1924 the *Aspen Daily Times* complained about "speed fiends" terrorizing the streets of the city, and within a year the first vehicular fatality occurred. Then, to the joy of beleaguered Aspenities, the Hope, Midnight, and Aspen Mines reported "good strikes." The year was 1929. In October the stock market collapsed. The entire nation went into a terrible economic tailspin. Almost every mine in the Aspen region closed. Even more people packed up their belongings and left town.

The 1930 Colorado State Business Directory pegged Aspen's population at 1,265. Locals knew that it hovered closer to 700. Aspen's mining days were over. After a half century, the silver gods had finally deserted the city. Now what? Some contended that Aspen's best chance for economic salvation lie in summer tourism. Others in the Roaring Fork Valley continued to put their faith in cattle and crops. A few maverick dreamers had other ideas. They championed snow and intellectualism.

Snow, a savior? From the moment the first prospector set foot in the valley, snow had been the enemy. Prospectors abhorred it, animals struggled through it, train engines ground to a halt in it, automobiles got stuck in it, merchants cursed it, and roofs collapsed under its weight. That snow could ever be part of the town's economic revival must have struck locals as the pinnacle of irony. The

Looking North on Galena Street Aspen, Colo.

dreamers remained resolute. Why not take advantage of Aspen's snowy mountain terrain — with so much of it uniquely suited for skiing? Skiing and Aspen were a perfect match. Skeptics knew that for decades miners had rigged utilitarian wooden skis to travel from one place to another. Admittedly, on rare occasions they swooped and hollered their way down steep slopes, but how could there be any money in that? There was, insisted the ski advocates, some of them 10th Mountain Ski Division veterans who during World War II had trained at Camp Hale south of Leadville. The time was ripe. Once aroused out of its economic doldrums, they insisted that the Crystal City could become a skiing Mecca. Although few locals openly criticized such bold notions, most harbored doubts.

Intellectualism, another savior? Few residents could even spell the elitist-sounding word. Most miners did not know what it meant. Even those locals who understood the concept must have wondered how the exercise of thinking abstractly or profoundly could possibly improve the Crystal City's economic fortunes. Again, a few maverick dreamers remained resolute. What better place to discuss intellectual issues than in a invigorating mountain environment — far away from the daily mind-numbing responsibilities and minutia? Anyone who has hiked along an untrammeled stretch of mountain stream, meandered through an alpine

meadow flush with wild flowers, or sat on top of a mountain ridge amid indescribable natural grandeur knows it inspires thought. So why not bring together some of the world's most distinguished scholars and humanitarians to seek understanding and exchange ideas in Aspen's alpine majesty? Aspen and intellectualism, another perfect match. Although many locals did not immediately warm to plans for such high-sounding academic seminars and symposia, if it meant money in their pockets, they were willing to sit back and see what happened.

In this final chapter the tale of how snow and intellectualism started Aspen on its trajectory toward becoming a world-class tourist, intellectual, and cultural center unfolds. It is as fascinating as it is unlikely. As for skiing, new technologies and America's changing leisure patterns following World War II contributed significantly to Aspen's dizzying success. That tourists also started to flock to Aspen during the summer months seemed only natural. Summer recreational opportunities abounded in the mountains and Roaring Fork Valley. As for intellectualism, it thrived for different reasons. A few concerned people knowingly, and at times arrogantly, addressed issues that profoundly effected the post World War II psyche. Remember, in the 1940s humans faced the unspeakable horrors of concentration camps and the specter of a thermonuclear monster wiping out all life systems. (The psychological fallout from those terrifying human creations remains with us to this day.) Soon other groups — musicians, photographers, architects, and athletes, among others — chose lofty Aspen as a gathering place as well. In short, although unlikely partners, snow and intellectualism combined to thrust Aspen into the world's spotlight. The Crystal City had finally found its saviors.

221

Eerily vacant streets

A deserted downtown Aspen on a wintry day in the early 1920s. (Denver Public Library, Western History Department)

Engineer's License, Aspen Quarantined, Gum Shoes, and Deadly Tornados

Tuesday, February 3, 1920. Sent $15⁰⁰ to the Board of Engineer Examiners at Denver for a license as Engineer. The board of health quarantined the town & closed everything up. Schools too. Fine warm day.

Friday, February, 6, 1920. Bought pair of gum shoes for $1.50 at Kobey's. Engaged a team to go down the river tomorrow to do some work for the county.

Wednesday, April 21, 1920. Stormy day. I was home all day. About a foot of new snow fell since yesterday morning. Bad storm all over the west & tornadoes in Miss. & Alabama. Lots of people killed. (Armstrong's journals)

Still clinging to silver

*I*n 1917, the Park Tunnel Mining and Milling Company was established to tap into the Tourtelotte Park ore reserves. In 1920, the company discovered a six-foot vein of ore containing 13,902 ounces of silver per ton. Fiscal faith in the discovery resulted in construction of a 7,000-foot tram to transport the silver-rich ore down Aspen Mountain. It cost $40,000. The lower Park Tunnel Tram building (now part of the Tipple Lodge) is shown here.

For decades tramways (top right) ferried ore down to Aspen. Miners road the ore buckets (bottom) back and forth to the mines. (Courtesy of Adeline Zupancis Kirsten) (Courtesy of Leo Stambaugh) (Courtesy of Ben Kirsten)

Tearing Down A Brewery, Animals Skins, Assisted Suicide, and A Splendid Rainbow

Wednesday, May 5, 1920. *Went over to Pete Olson's to see him & Dan McArthur. Pete is helping tear down Cris Sander's brewery. Dan has 7 fox skins, one martin, & 12 weasel skins. Dan came over home with me & got some parsnips & carrots. I got a bottle of Hotstetters Bitters for $1.25.*

Saturday, June 5, 1920. *Left the house at 6.30 am. Rode in an Auto. Surveyed strip of land for a country road. Park helped Charlie Warner shoot himself this P.M. in Red Butte Cemetery on his wife's grave.*

Wednesday, June 23, 1920. *I took a walk up Castle Creek this P.M. I never saw the choke cherries blooming as luxuriant as they are now. The wild roses are just coming in bloom. The girls are out picking them along the R.R.. Mrs. Flagg was buried this P.M. Very fine, warm day. A splendid rainbow this evening.* (Armstrong's journals)

Tramway stock

Aspen businessman John Zupancis purchased 75 shares of capitol stock in The Park Tunnel Tramway Company in 1921. Like most investors, he lost his money. (Courtesy of Ben Kirsten)

224

Appropriately named?

Members of the Beck family stand by the Hope Mine shaft house. In 1922, The Hope Mining and Leasing Company reported a balance of $131.13. As for this mine paying off big, there appeared to be little hope. (Courtesy of the Beck family collection)

225

Taking stock

*B*efore embarking on their tour, the Board of Directors of the Hope Mine pose in horse-drawn ore carts at the mine entrance. One wonders how much stock (right) these men held in their own mine. All the board members are wearing rain slickers and rain hats, a sure sign of dripping water down under. Many of the board members grasp long miners' candles. Empty wooden candle boxes are strewn in the foreground. (Denver Public Library, Western History Department) (Courtesy of Ralph Kemper)

226

227

Mining no more

Dilapidated mining structures stand lonely watches over abandoned mine dumps. By the 1930s this scene at the Little Annie Mine (above) repeated itself throughout most of the once-booming Aspen mining district. (Denver Public Library, Western History Department)

Snowmass, Mistaken Identity, A Big Strike, Jack Dempsey, and Moonshine

Saturday, July 10, 1920. Rode down to Snowmass in an auto to survey an addition to county road. Could not find any corner to tie to. So we came back to Woody & surveyed an addition to width of county road of 40 feet. Park helped me. It was in an alfalfa field & the mosquitoes were very bad. Rained on us. We got home 8.30 in the evening. Had a great ride.

Thursday, August, 12, 1920. Took a sack of lettuce to Nate Larson. While there, a great excitement broke out. People discovered a bear on West Aspen Mountain. Jim Gould took his rifle & shot it and low & behold it was a black sheep. A crowd of women & kids congregated to see the bear.

Monday, February 28, 1921. Fine. Parke & I were up to see Nate Larson. I bought a dozen eggs for 40c. By the Humdinger, they have made a big strike of high grade ore in the Hope Tunnel, and the stock has gone to $2^{50} per share. I hope it is so.

Saturday, July 2, 1921. Warm. I spent $1.35 for grub. Dempsey knocked out Carpenter in the 4th round at Jersey City. Irrigating my spuds.

Wednesday, September 21, 1921. Took a walk with Park over to the Cowenhoven tunnel & the Hunter-creek mill. Things are lively over there. Very fine day. Had frost this morning.

Tuesday, November 29, 1921. I am 74 years old today. Fine day.

Tuesday, July 4, 1922. Was up town this forenoon taking in the celebration. Saw Bob Carson, an oldtimer who drove stage to Ashcroft 35 or 40 years ago.

Tuesday, August 29, 1922. Rode up to the cabin this evening with Bob Davey in his car. Got there about 6. Found the cabin allright. Somebody changed fish rods on me. Left a broken one in place of my good one. Also got away with my cedar bucket that I have had for 40 years. Darn'em

Tuesday, Christmas — December 25, 1923. Julius Zupancis called yesterday evening & gave me a nice lot of groceries for Christmas. Frank Henry Jr. brought me some Turkey pie & c this evening.

Sunday, February 10, 1924. Fair day. George Brum was here the most of the day visiting. Sam Sweeney says that government prohibition agents arrested 4 citizens of Aspen for moonshining last evening.

Thursday, May 8, 1924. I have neglected my diary shamefully.

Saturday, June 21, 1924. Kenneth Harrison & Jack Leahy called 2 AM full with a qt. Hot day in sun. Froze ice on my tub yesterday morning. I had my beans covered, so they were allright.

Thursday, October 9, 1924. Fine day. George Brum's house burned today A total loss. Too bad. I am sorry.

Sunday, September 13, 1925. Park rustled a pair of crutches for me yesterday.

Friday, October 9, 1925. Fine day. Two Prohibition men in town yesterday. Fined Bob Davy [?] $250 & cash $17 and 10 days jail.

Friday, December 25, 1925. Christmas Day. Ralph Myers brought me a fine dinner. Fine day. (Armstrong's journals)

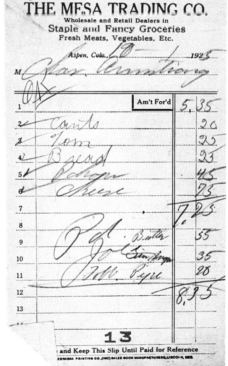

Struggling to stay

During the 1920s and 1930s, those who remained in Aspen had to work hard to earn enough money to stay in their beloved city. Most of them never experienced the boom days. None of their children did. Shown here (center) is Julius Zupancis's Mesa Trading Company and a portion of one of his calendars (top). His 1933 Plymouth van's spare-wheel cover sports an ad for a local garage. Charles Armstrong often bought food at the Mesa Trading Company (right). (Courtesy of Ben Kirsten) (Courtesy of Adeline Zupancis Kirsten) (Armstrong's journals)

On their wedding day

*J*ulius and Mary Zupancis look into the camera on their wedding day. Their visages bespeak a gentleness and caring that reflected their reputations in Aspen. (Courtesy of Adeline Zupancis Kirsten)

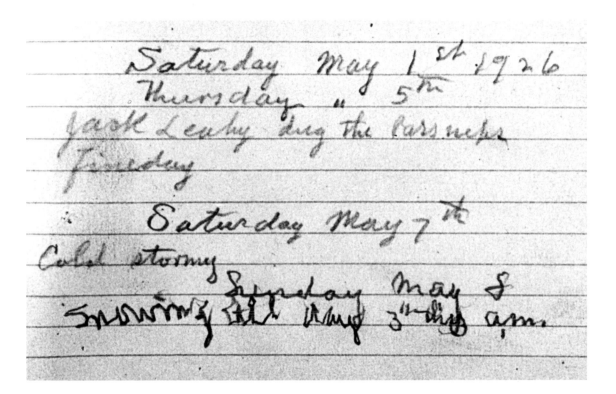

Snowing all day

After spending almost forty-six years in the Aspen area, Charles Armstrong scribbled his last journal entry on May 7, 1926. His labored writing style may indicate that he suffered a stroke, although the fate of the Charles S. Armstrong remains unknown. Searches through Aspen newspapers and cemetery lists in Aspen and Arkport have failed to reveal the fate of this man to whom this author owes so much. (Armstrong's journals)

THE HOTEL JEROME MANSOR S. ELISHA, Proprietor

**Thoroughly Modern Rooms
One of the few Good Hotels
in Colorado**

AMERICAN PLAN
SAMPLE ROOMS

Luxury, Without Extravagance.
Everybody's Home. Beautiful
Mountain Scenery. Fishing. Hunt-
ing. A delightful place for a
Summer Vacation.

**Billiard Hall, Barber Shop and
Confectionery in Connection.**

Phone 33   Aspen, Colo.

Hotel Jerome: Phone 33

During the 1920s and 1930s, not many people rang up the Hotel Jerome (left) at the intersection of South Mill Street and East Main Street. Touted in the 1930 Colorado State Business Directory (above) as "One of the few Good Hotels in Colorado," it failed to attract many tourists.

In 1926, there might have been more dogs than humans in Aspen. One summer visitor complained: "You could kill off at least a hundred dogs and still have plenty. I never saw so many dogs in one town before in all my travels" (quoted by Fredrick, 1999). (Author's collection) (Denver Public Library, Western History Department)

"*The Aspen Times* For Sale: Cheap for Cash"

On December 5, 1930, *The Aspen Times* ran its own "For Sale" ad (right). This "One Big Opportunity for a Newspaper Man" failed to attract a buyer. Not much cash flowed anywhere in the United States, let alone in Aspen, during the Great Depression. The town's only bank, The Aspen State Bank (above), soon closed. (Both courtesy of Adeline Zupancis Kirsten)

234

Looking back for salvation

Aspenites clung to hope for renewed mining glory. Who could blame them? Aspen was born a mining town and could be reborn a mining town. But it was not to be. Regardless of *The Aspen Times's* optimistic rhetoric, mining would not rescue the Crystal City from economic ruination. (Both courtesy of Adeline Zupancis Kirsten)

ASPEN, PITKIN COUNTY, COLORADO, FRIDAY, FEBRUARY 7, 1930

ASPEN GETTING READY TO BOOM

Next week Mr. D. P. Rohlfing will put a force of men to work laying air pipes throughout the Spar Consolidated properties reaching from the A. J. to the Aspen ground.

As soon as the air can shoot through the pipes the machine drills will start ripping up the ore chutes and the muckers and trammers will shoot it out to the surface.

One of the experts of the American Smelting & Refining company has already looked over the ore situation in the Aspen district and has okayed every statement made by Mr. Rohlfing "that Aspen has unlimited ore bodies that only need developing to repay the developers a thousand-fold."

It is the prediction of The Times that the A. S. & R. will back their expert's report to the limit and that means putting Aspen back on the mining map.

235

The only Aspen they knew

*F*ive-year-old Adeline Zupancis, the smallest of the two girls standing in front, pose for the camera in front of St. Mary's Catholic Church during a confirmation in 1930. She and Peggy Healy, the girl standing next to her, led the confirmation group.

These children only knew an impoverished Aspen. Yet as a child Adeline loved the small-town atmosphere and the abundant recreational opportunities. She also felt safe. (Courtesy of Adeline Zupancis Kirsten)

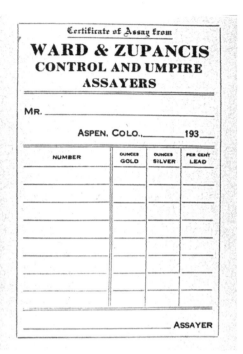

Certificate of Assay from

WARD & ZUPANCIS
CONTROL AND UMPIRE
ASSAYERS

MR. _____

ASPEN, COLO.,_____193___

NUMBER	OUNCES GOLD	OUNCES SILVER	PER CENT LEAD

_____ ASSAYER

236

Looking North on Galena Street, Aspen, Colo.

He did not want to leave

John Zupancis owned the Conoco Station (top right) on the corner of Main Street and Galena Street in the early 1930s. Much to his, and many of their friends' disappointment, there was not enough business to support a growing family. In 1937 John Zupancis and his family departed for Grass Valley, California. There he managed a Shell gas station (bottom right). His daughter, Adeline, still cherishes some of the Zupancis family stationery and a small match folder from their Aspen days. (Top right: Author's collection) (Others courtesy of Adeline Zupancis Kirsten)

103 E. MAIN ST., CORNER GALENA   P.O. BOX 175

IN ACCOUNT WITH
JOHN ZUPANCIS
FILLING STATION
ASPEN, COLO.

M_____

_____

_____

JOHN J. ZUPANCIS

⁓

ASPEN, COLORADO

Even more quiet in Ashcroft

*I*n the late 1930s, a man climbs into the rumble seat of his 1934 Ford while his dog keeps watch. The old Ashcroft Hotel (and probably brothel) stands vacant in the background. This historic two-story structure with rectangular bays and a false front modified to include a center gable has been partially restored by the Aspen Historical Society. During summer months, Aspen Historical Society interns conduct tours of the long-abandoned settlement. (Denver Public Library, Western History Department)

Dog sledding and "Sergeant Preston of the Yukon"

*T*he archival description of top left photograph reads: "Dog sledding near old ghost town of Ashcroft." A team of seven pairs of Toklat Husky dogs pull a sled with a male driver (probably Stuart Mace) with two women skiers in tow near the remains of the once-booming mining camp. In 1948 Stuart Mace, a World War II veteran and commander of a canine division, brought his family and this dog sled operation to Ashcroft (top right).

If these images evoke memories of the popular early television series, "Sergeant Preston of the Yukon," they should. They filmed the series near Ashcroft. (Denver Public Library, Western History Department)

Access to matchless mountain scenery

*A*spen always had its matchless mountain
scenery. What most people in
Colorado and the rest of the United States
did not have was independent, easy access to
it. That all began to change with the advent
of the automobile, improved roads, and
state highways. By the mid-1930s people
from large population centers, like Denver,
could drive to Leadville along Highway 24
(top right), then over Independence Pass to
Aspen on Highway 82 (bottom right), to
dramatic Snowmass Lake (left). America's
love affair with the automobile seemed
strongest in the mountains, where one
could combine adventure, freedom, and
breathtaking mountain landscapes.
(Highway sign: Courtesy of Dave
Hungenberg) (Postcard and *The Aspen
Times* ad: Courtesy of Adeline Zupancis
Kirsten)

OLD and NEW
Road Around the Cliffs on
INDEPENDENCE
HIGHWAY Over the Top of the World..

Independence Pass Highway

During late summer and fall, Aspen families, like the Becks and Zupancises, drove their vehicles (above) to the top of Independence Pass. Adeline Zupancis Kirsten recalls that: "it was quite an adventure, with all those steep drop-offs and everything." Right, her father John Zupancis strikes a confident pose next to his 1921 Dodge on the way to the summit. (Courtesy of the Beck family collection) (Courtesy of Adeline Zupancis Kirsten)

On the Continental Divide

*A*deline Zupancis Kirsten (third from left) stands among family members and friends on top of Independence Pass in 1941. Sixty-one years earlier Charles S. Armstrong passed near this spot on his way to Aspen and Roaring Fork City. Now modern vehicles speed over the summit on a paved Highway 82, except during winter months when snow renders it impassable. (Courtesy of Adeline Zupancis Kirsten)

241

Hardscrabble Hill, Taylor Pass, near Aspen Colo.
Note pine tree tied to Auto for Drag

Dragging a tree, but not for Christmas

*M*ore adventuresome automobile enthusiasts tackled "Hard Scrabble Hill," near Taylor Pass above Ashcroft. Above, they had tied a pine tree to the rear of their 1924 Ford Model T for "drag," meaning the conifer helped brake the vehicle on steep downhill portions of the route. (Courtesy of the Beck family collection)

Fewer trains, but more cars

By the 1940s, fewer trains, but more cars rolled into Aspen. Above, a Denver and Rio Grande Western train approaches Aspen on June 23, 1942. Longtime Roaring Fork Valley resident and "Police Judge" Charlie Case took his personally labeled trunk (left) on train and automobile trips. (Denver Public Library, Western History Department) (Courtesy of Ken and Jackie Broughton)

Rodeo parade

Against the backdrop of Aspen Mountain and the Wheeler Opera House, horses and riders parade down Main Street. The front of a 1947 Buick protrudes behind a 1946 Chevrolet. In the foreground a boy peddles his bicycle by an abandoned gas pump in a vacant lot. In 1941, Loretta Love (right) returned to Aspen with the John Zupancis family to lead a band in the always popular Fourth of July parade. (Denver Public Library, Western History Department) (Courtesy of Adeline Zupancis Kirsten)

245

"Half House"

*I*n the 1940s, lonely homes (left) lined once-bustling Aspen streets. Dubbed the "Half House," this unusual edifice now occupies 218 North Monarch Street. After extensive remodeling, it no longer looks like its nickname. Jackie and Ken Broughton salvaged a ornate stained-glass window (top) in an abandoned and dilapidated house before it was broken by vandals. (Courtesy of Leo Stambaugh) (Courtesy of Jackie and Ken Broughton)

Victorian elegance

 246

uilt in the early 1890s by J. W. Atkinson, part owner of the Little Annie Mine, this Queen Anne-style Victorian home (right) on 125 East Main Street served as a mortuary in the 1970s. Various persons, including Tom Sardy, a local business partner with Walter Paepcke and owner of the Aspen Lumber and Supply Company, have owned the house. Aspen Airport's "Sardy Field" is named after Tom. Now the elegant home is owned by a group of investors and operated as the Sardy House Bed and Breakfast. (Courtesy of Leo Stambaugh)

Nothing but piles of snow

*I*n the late 1930s, winter in Aspen meant nothing put bothersome piles of snow. Barely a tourist could be found. One or two mines opened, then closed. Left, a large industrial scoop and a boiler part lay in the snow on Smuggler Mountain. A small abandoned brick building stands like a lonely sentinel, gazing forlornly upon the nearly abandoned mountain city. The Hotel Jerome and Wheeler Opera House comprise the only two familiar landmarks. (Denver Public Library, Western History Department)

247

"How it all ended in Aspen"

What better visual metaphor for a failed mining camp that once held such great promise? Here stands Henry Gillespie's — one of Aspen's most prominent mining pioneer's — vacant, cold home. Weeds dominate the long-neglected yard, window casings in the towers are crumbling, and numerous window panes are missing. In the mid-1930s, this somber, yet poignant image might have carried the caption, "How it all ended in Aspen." (Denver Public Library, Western History Department)

HISTORIC ASPEN IN RARE PHOTOGRAPHS

Then came more people, this time with skis

Aspen did not become a ski Mecca overnight. For over a half century Aspenites (see page 134) enjoyed utilitarian skiing in the Aspen vicinity. In the late 1930s and early 1940s, it was the scale and purpose of skiing that changed dramatically. Most people acknowledge Tom Flynn, a miner's son, as the father of Aspen skiing.

In the spring of 1936 in California, of all places, Flynn's chance meeting with Olympic bobsled champion Billy Fiske resulted in the creation of the Highland-Bavarian Corporation. The fledgling company decided to make Mount Hayden near Ashcroft the focus of their ski-development efforts. "But Aspen [right], not Ashcroft, was to become synonymous with unexcelled snow and outstanding terrain. Flynn enticed Andre Roch, the celebrated Swiss mountaineer and downhill champion, to design a ski run on Aspen Mountain. This became the famous Roch Run" (Pearce and Eflin, 1990). (Denver Public Library, Western History Department)

249

250

Primitive and fun

This view from the 1930s shows six winter enthusiasts sitting across one another as their "boat tow" is dragged up Aspen Mountain. Vehicle tracks can be seen in the snow. (Denver Public Library, Western History Department)

HISTORIC ASPEN IN RARE PHOTOGRAPHS

A ski jump and ski runs are born

Although Aspen still maintains some of its original charm, it is hard to imagine this idyllic winter scene now. In the foreground an old horse-drawn wagon seems to be looking at the first ski jump and ski runs on Aspen Mountain, wondering what will become of all this. (Colorado Historical Society, Stephen Hart Library)

251

Technology, travel, and leisure

*I*mproved skiing technology, easier highway access, and the changing face of American leisure activities soon attracted winter crowds to Aspen that rivaled the early mining boom-day hoards. One of the first "ski trains" pulled into Aspen in 1937.

Soon ski teams from across the country came to take advantage of the magnificent Aspen slopes and the ultra-modern ski lifts (left). The Northwestern University girls ski team paid $2 a night to stay at the Roaring Fork Hotel (below). Most importantly for the locals, skiers came to leave silver in Aspen, not take it out. (Colorado Historical Society, Stephen Hart Library) (Author's collection)

253

Ever bigger and better

T hree years after Aspen hosted the Rocky Mountain Ski Association Championship in 1938, the Aspen Ski Club put on the U. S. World Alpine Championship. This put Aspen on the international skiing map. From then on, except for a respite during World War II, everything about Aspen skiing got bigger and better. Even summer months meant more ski-construction activity (above, probably in the early 1950s). (Denver Public Library, Western History Department)

254

Another ski pioneer and the world's longest chair lift

After World War II, Friedl Pfeifer (above), a member of the 10th Mountain Division, convinced Walter Paepcke (see page 257) to invest even more capital in the burgeoning Aspen ski business. As a result, by 1947 Aspen could brag about having the world's longest chair lift (right), called simply, "Lift #1." This "modern" lift featured footrests, armrests, safety bars and — when temperatures plummeted — burlap covers for skiers' comfort during the half hour ride to the top. (Author's collection) (Colorado Historical Society, Stephen Hart Library)

255

Up, up, and away!

Charles Bradley of the U.S. Army 10th Mountain Division soars up, up, and away! What better visual metaphor for the Aspen's skiing prospects? (Denver Public Library, Western History Department)

More than skiing

*T*he booming ski business soon led to the rebirth of downtown Aspen. In 1947, *apres'* skiers, and others, gathered at the Red Onion (right) to discuss the day's adventure and enjoy the bracing alpine climate under crystal clear skies. In 1949 the Wheeler Opera House (upper left) re-opened with Burl Ives giving the inaugural performance. The average cost of a town lot rose to about $100 (Fredrick, 1999). (Denver Public Library, Western History Department)

256

An early Who's Who

Smiling for the camera is a row of early movers and shakers in Aspen. The money, confidence, and imagination of Walter Paepcke and his wife gave impetus to Aspen's incredible trajectory of financial and cultural success. This photograph carries the following caption: **"They put Aspen back on the map:** 'Chuck' Bishop, Hotel Jerome manager; Walter Paepcke, Chicago millionaire who led the move; Mrs. Paepcke; Mrs. Bishop; Mrs. Herbert Bayer, wife of the designer; ski star Dick Durrance; Mrs. Durrance; Len Woods, executive secretary of Federation Internationale de Ski; Fred Iselin and Friedl Pfeifer, who head the Aspen Ski School." (Author's collection)

Remodeling the town

*T*he caption on this picture proclaims: "**Hebert Bayer,** who 'styled' Aspen for Paepcke, stands before an example of 'bastard miners' architecture — pale yellow house with white trim." This house still stands and is considered one of Aspen's finest Victorian homes. (Author's collection)

258

Dancing in the streets

B y the late 1940s, Aspenites had good reason to dance in the streets. With the venerable Hotel Jerome in the background, couples dance along Main Street during a Fourth of July parade. (Courtesy of Leo Stambaugh) (Upper and lower right: Courtesy of Adeline Zupancis Kirsten)

An elegant lobby and canine fixture

*T*he refurbished Hotel Jerome's front lobby features a tile floor, sideboards, fireplace with mantel and mirror, supporting pillars with leafy capitals, leather sofa, armchairs, and other elegant trappings. Bingo, Fred Iselin's 180-pound St. Bernard, often sat on the sidewalk in front of the Hotel Jerome. Bingo also turned a few heads while ascending Aspen Mountain on the ski lift. (Courtesy of Leo Stambaugh) (Author's collection)

Rates American Plan (including meals)

HOTEL ROOMS *per day*

	single occupancy	double occupancy
Without private bath	$ 8 - $ 9	$ 7 - $ 9 per person
With private toilet	$10 - $11	$ 8 - $ 9 per person
With connecting bath	$10 - $11	$ 8 - $11 per person
With private bath	$10 - $12	$ 8 - $12 per person
Deluxe Bedrooms and Suites (bedroom, bath and small sitting room)	$14 - $18.50	$11 - $15 per person

COTTAGES *per day*

	single occupancy	double occupancy
Cottage rooms sharing bath	$ 9 - $12	$ 7 - $10 per person
Cottage rooms private bath	$10 - $25	$ 9 - $12 per person

Rates European Plan

ASPEN BLOCK ROOMS *per day*

	single occupancy	double occupancy
Rooms with private bath and kitchenette	$8 - $10	$ 5 - $ 7.50 per person

ROARING FORK ROOMS *per day*

Dormitory type rooms accommodating 4 to 6 persons per room	$2.00 per person

Reservations are held only until 6:00 p.m. of the proposed date of arrival.

261

"Rates American Plan (including meals): Double Occupancy, $7-$9 per room"

*H*otel Jerome guests dress for dinner. No one seems to care that the ceiling still shows water stains after years of neglect. (Courtesy of Leo Stambaugh) (Courtesy of Adeline Zupancis Kirsten)

Frontiersmen's Bar

*T*hirsty Hotel Jerome guests drink their favorite liquid refreshments beneath illustrated ads for Blue Jeans, beer, and who knows what else? The man on the right with argyle socks appears to have had enough to drink. (Courtesy of Leo Stambaugh)

An outdoor pool, too

This Hotel Jerome pool scene would have had the first prospectors in the Roaring Fork Valley scratching the back of their heads. Swimmers relax in lounge chairs while a woman in a plaid skirt strolls by. Signs on the changing room doors read "Massage Women" and "Massage Men, Please Knock." The Pitkin County Courthouse watches over the leisure summer proceedings. (Denver Public Library, Western History Department)

263

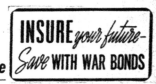

Aspen, Silver City of the Silver State; Scenic Wonderland; All-Year Sportsman's Paradise

INSURE *your future—* *Save* WITH WAR BONDS

The Aspen Times

VOLUME 64   NO. 10   ASPEN, COLORADO   Thursday, March 8, 1945   EVERY FRIDAY MORNING

"All-Year Sportsman Paradise"

*I*n the mid-1940s, an illustrated masthead of *The Aspen Daily Times* highlights three of Aspen's greatest assets: skiing, scenery, and fishing. (Courtesy of Adeline Zupancis Kirsten)

Adapting to the times

O ld local businesses, and some new ones, happily catered to tourists' recreational needs. Lewis H. Tomkins Hardware Company (bottom) embraced fishing supplies. Left, a lone fisherman wets his line in the Roaring Fork River. (Courtesy of Leo Stambaugh) (Courtesy of Adeline Zupancis Kirsten)

265

Ascending the cliffs

Rock climbers came to Aspen as well. Some honed their mountaineering skills "at altitude" in preparation for more challenging ascents throughout the world. Aspen Street can be seen in the right foreground. Shadow Mountain looms in the background. (Courtesy of Leo Stambaugh)

266

Young cowboys and cowgirls

With grand mountain vistas for backdrops, parents and children alike enjoyed horseback riding in the Aspen vicinity. The Aspen Rodeo Grounds also held informal rodeos for young riders (above). (Courtesy of Leo Stambaugh)

Gary Cooper at the Four Seasons Archery Club

268

Aspen also attracted popular actors. Right, Gary Cooper removes an arrow from a target tacked to a bale of hay at the Four Seasons Archery Club (formerly the Newman Mine). (Courtesy of Leo Stambaugh)

Tennis anyone?

*A*s if skiing, hiking, fishing, hunting, camping, mountain climbing, and archery were not enough, one could also play tennis on the Four Seasons's new courts. The Newman Mine manager's house became the "clubhouse." To most, Aspen now truly had it all. Yet the academic seminars, symposia, and major fine arts festivals were still to come. (This location is now part of the Aspen Music Festival and School Campus.) (Courtesy of Leo Stambaugh)

GOETHE Bicentennial Convocation and Music Festival 1949

Aspen, Colorado U.S.A.
June 27–July 16

270

Toward a "Universal Man"

*C*hicago industrialist Walter Paepcke and his wife Elizabeth (see page 257) fell in love with Aspen during their brief stay in 1945. Soon they made Aspen their permanent home. Walter Paepcke also saw its potential to contribute to his dream of "a community of peace with opportunities for a man's complete life . . . where he can earn a living, profit by healthy, physical recreation, with facilities at hand for his enjoyment of art, music, and education" (quoted in Pearce and Elfin, 1990).

Walter Paepcke's vision of a "Universal Man" inspired the first Goethe Bicentennial Convention and Music Festival (left) in July, 1949. (Author's collection)

GOETHE,
AN ETCHING
BY LIPS

Honoring Goethe's intellect

T he narrative in the first Goethe Bicentennial program (above) elucidates the high-sounding purpose of the gathering. Over 2,000 attendees from around the world descended on Aspen for this cerebral event. Hence, once again Aspen attracted the attention of the United States and the international community. (Both from author's collection)

272

Under the big top

A huge tent (left) designed by Euro Saarine is erected for $60,000 for the first Goethe Bicentennial Festival. Invited guests include Arthur Rubinstein (inset), Thorton Wilder, Jose Ortega y Gassett, and the entire Minneapolis Symphony (bottom). (All from author's collection)

The most honored guest

"To provide a central orientation to Goethe's place in the 20th century, **Dr. Albert Schweitzer,** philosopher-doctor-musician-theologian — acknowledged throughout the civilized world as the foremost modern disciple of Goethe — has consented to journey to the United States for the first time in his life. He will present the main lecture at the International Goethe Convocation" (The Goethe Bicentennial program, 1949). Right, humanitarian Schweitzer speaks with other guests. Schweitzer never returned to America.

The success of this intellectual and musical celebration "lead to the continuation of the Aspen Music Festival and the development of the Aspen Institute for Humanistic Studies, the Aspen Physics Institute, the Music Associates of Aspen, and the Aspen Music School. The present Music Tent and the 'international style' architecture of the Aspen Institute were created by the noted Bauhaus designer Herbert Bayer, assisted by Aspen architect Fritz Benedict" (Pearce and Eflin, 1999). (Aspen Historical Society)

273

274

The essence of Aspen

*I*n Aspen, mining prospered, then disappeared. Although today it seems unimaginable, skiing and festivals may someday disappear as well. No matter, the essence of Aspen lies in the majestic beauty that encompasses it. As long as that essence is not completely compromised, Aspen will survive. (Courtesy of Leo Stambaugh)

What would Charles S. Armstrong say?

*I*f Charles S. Armstrong could return to the remote high country, like the head of Difficult Creek above Ashcroft, he would not notice much difference since he entered the area in 1880. For that he would probably be thankful. As for strolling through modern downtown Aspen, that might also please him. Armstrong always craved being part of Aspen's prosperity and excitement. That is why he came to the majestic Roaring Fork Valley. (Courtesy of Leo Stambaugh)

275

Abbott, D. (1989). *Colorado Midland Railway, Daylight Through the Divide Denver,* Colorado: Sundance Publications.

Aspen City Directories (1885 - 1930).

Athearn, R. G. (1962). *Rebel of the Rockies, A History of the Denver and Rio Grande Western Railroad.* New Haven, Connecticut: Yale University Press.

Bancroft, C. (1954). *Famous Aspen.* Denver, Colorado: The Golden Press.

Barlow-Perez, S. (1991). *A History of Aspen.* Aspen, Colorado: Who Press.

Black Elk Speaks: *Being the Life Story of a Holy Man of the Oglala Souix* (as told through John G. Neihardt). (1932: 1995 reprint). Lincoln, Nebraska: University of Nebraska Press.

Blair, E. (1980). *Leadville: Colorado's Magic City.* Boulder, Colorado: Pruett Publishing Company.

Buys, C. J. (1986). "Accounts of the Battle at Milk Creek: Implications for Historical Accuracy." *Essays and Monographs in Colorado History,* 4, 59 - 80.

Buys, C. J. (1986). "Power in the Mountains: Lucien Nunn Catapults the San Juans into the Age of Electricity." *Colorado Heritage,* 4, 25 - 37.

Buys, C. J. (1993). "Fort Crawford: A Symbol of Transition." *Journal of the Western Slope,* 8 (2), 1 - 29.

Buys, C. J. (1997). *Historic Leadville in Rare Photographs and Drawings.* Ouray, Colorado: Western Reflections, Inc.

Buys, C. J. (1997: Summer). "Of Frozen Fire Hydrants and 'Drunkin' Sons of a Bitches,' Early Leadville's Volunteer Firemen." *Colorado Heritage,* 2 - 15.

Buys, C. J. (1998: Summer). "Henry M. Teller: Colorado's 'Silver Senator,'" *Colorado Heritage,* 29 - 36.

Buys, C. J. (1998). *Historic Telluride in Rare Photographs.* Ouray, Colorado: Western Reflections, Inc.

Buys, C. J. (1999). *Illustrations of Historic Colorado.* Ouray, Colorado: Western Reflections, Inc.

Canfield, J. G. (1893). *Mines and Mining Men of Colorado.* Denver, Colorado: John G. Canfield Publishing.

Coleman, J. T. (1997). *The Skeletal Shell Game: A History of a Colorado Ghost Town, 1880- Present.* Unpublished master's thesis, University of Colorado, Boulder, Colorado.

Crane, W. H. (1913). *In the Rocky Mountains with the Indian, Bear & Wolf.* Denver, Colorado: The Smith-Brooks Printing Company.

Crofutt, G. A. (1881). *Crofutt's Grip-Sack Guide of Colorado.* Omaha, Nebraska: Overland Publishing, Co.

Crofutt, G. A. (1885). *Crofutt's Grip-Sack Guide of Colorado.* Omaha, Nebraska: Overland Publishing, Co.

Daily, K. K. and Guenin, G. T. (1994). *Aspen, The Quiet Years (1910 - 1930).* Aspen, Colorado: Red Ink, Inc.

Dill, R. G. (1881). "History of Lake County" in *History of the Arkansas Valley,* Colorado. Chicago, Illinois: Baskin and Co.

Fredrick, L. (1999). "Time Line History of Aspen." Aspen Historical Society.

Glover, J. (1969). *The "Bobbed Wire" Bible.* Sunset, Texas. Sunset Trading Post.

Hafen, L. and Hafen, A. (1948). *Colorado: A Story of the State and Its People.* Denver, Colorado: Old West Publishing Company.

Hall, F. (1889 - 1895). *History of the State of Colorado.* Volumes 1 - 4. Chicago, Illinois: The Blakely Printing Company

Hallett Letterpress Book. (1995). Aspen Historical Society (Larry Fredrick).

Landry, J. and Lane, J. (1972). *"Horsethief" Kelley and His Camera.* Private printing.

Miller, M. E. (1997). *Hollow Victory: The White River Expedition of 1879 and the Battle of Milk Creek.* Niwot, Colorado: University of Colorado Press.

O'Rear, J. and O'Rear, F. (1966). *The Aspen Story, Including Skiing the Aspen Way.* New York, New York, A. S. Barnes.

Pearce, S. and Eflin, R. (1990). *A Guide to Historic Aspen and the Roaring Fork Valley.* Evergreen, Colorado: Cordillera Press, Inc. (Sponsored by the Aspen Historic Trust)

Pokagon, S. (1893). *The Red Man's Rebuke.* Hartford, Michigan: C. H. Engle.

Portrait and Biographical Record of the State of Colorado. (1899). Chicago, Illinois: Chapman Publishing Company.

Representative Men of Colorado in the Nineteenth Century. (1902). Denver, Colorado: The Rowell Art Publishing Company.

Rohrbough, M. J. (1986). *Aspen: The History of a Silver Mining Town, 1879 - 1893*. New York, New York: Oxford University Press.

Shoemaker, L. (1973: 3rd ed.) *Roaring Fork Valley, An Illustrated Chronicle*. Silverton, Colorado: Sundance Printing.

The Aspen Daily Chronicle (selected issues).

The Aspen Daily Leader (selected issues).

The Aspen Daily Times (selected issues).

The Rocky Mountain Sun (selected issues).

Wegman-French, L. (1990). *The History of The Holden-Marolt Site in Aspen, Colorado: The Holden Lixiviation Works, Farming and Ranching, and the Marolt Ranch 1879 - 1986*. Aspen Historical Society.

Wentworth, F. L. (1976). *Aspen on the Roaring Fork*. Denver, Colorado: Sundance Limited.

Wilson, J. (1999). *The Earth Shall Weep*. New York, New York: Atlantic Monthly Press.

Wood, S. (1889). *Over the Range to the Golden Gate*. Chicago, Illinois: R.R. Donnelly & Sons.

280

282

287

288